Winners have a plan, losers have an excuse

You don't beat a crisis –

– you beat your competitors

Marc Lammers

TIRION SPORT

MIX
Papier van verantwoorde herkomst
FSC® C004472
www.fsc.org

This book is published by
Tirion Uitgevers
PO Box 13288
3507 LG Utrecht
The Netherlands
Tirion is onderdeel van VBK | media

www.tirion.nl

Cover design: Hans Britsemmer, Kudelstaart
Cover photos: Ben Haeck (cover), Aschwin Snel (back)
Translation: Mike Wilkinson
Design (inside): ZetSpiegel, Best
Photos (inside): Ben Haeck, Jeroen van Bergen, Marc Lammers
With help from: Ton Hendrickx

ISBN 978 90 4391 355 3
ISBN e-book 978 90 4391 796 4
NUR 480

Vierde druk, 2017

Contents

Introduction: The biggest crisis

My biggest crisis? The Olympic final in Athens in 2004. Losing 2-1 to Germany. I cried for about three days. I thought, "See? I can't do it. I'll never be number one."
Most people would have been pleased with a silver medal. But we were after gold. We reckoned we had done everything we could for it. We had even beaten Germany 5-1 in the pool matches earlier in the Olympic tournament. Gold was there for the taking. The Dutch Olympic Committee had already prepared us for the celebratory reception at Holland Heineken House, our home in the Olympic Village, and the procedure – everything was already in place. Former internationals were going to be there to greet us, the previous women to win hockey gold medals for the Netherlands. After all, it was twenty years since the Dutch women's hockey team had won gold. We won the silver, but we lost the gold.

I seriously considered stopping. In my mind, I had in fact already quit. I had been able to get the Dutch women's hockey team up the world rankings from fourth place to second. And that was as far as it would go. Stopping at a low point.

Actually, I still feel sorry for the players on the losing side in the 2004 final who were no longer there in 2008. We missed gold in Athens because I was still too inexperienced then. If I had known then what I know now, that final would not have been lost. That still gnaws at me. That feeling of guilt is something I will never get rid of. Don't forget that the Dutch women's hockey team had only been the Olympic champions once before us, back in 1984.

Winners have a plan,
losers have an excuse

But I didn't stop. I used the crisis. I made the choice between fleeing and fighting. As a youngster, I had always chosen to stand my ground. Hockey was everything to me, and my talents lay in coaching. But now it had all changed. If you put everything on hold for four years, do everything to attain a single goal that you then fail to achieve, then giving up the struggle seems only logical.
Surely?

I decided to take up the gauntlet. To spend another four years building a team. To spend another four years aiming for Olympic gold. And we won gold at the Beijing Olympics in 2008. The crisis had been overcome. The ultimate proof. And then I did stop. At the top.

That victory in Beijing now allows me to look back at a process that took four years, or maybe even eight. From the low point to the high point. I beat the crisis.

Many of the experiences I went through, as well as the disappointments and the strategies, are equally applicable to crisis situations outside sport. In companies, within organisations, in families – in fact, wherever people come together and work together. How do you beat the crisis? Fight rather than flight. By reeling in that one target, little by little. By focusing on the process and not on the result. Because if the process is correct, the result will fall into place.

A crisis is perhaps the best period. It is precisely in a time of crisis, rather than in the 'good' times, that it is easier for you to stand out from your competitors. Because even the worst of the bunch can do well when times are easy. When things are difficult, it is all about who is the most creative and the cleverest. Those are the ones who will stand out from the crowd. Crisis situations kept stacking up throughout the run-up to the Olympics in China. Which is when I caught myself thinking something surprising. Whereas I could see other team managers

complaining and whingeing in the papers, I was thinking, "Yes, a crisis!"
A crisis is only a crisis if you say it is.

Until that point, it is a limitless source of inspiration, energy and challenges.

Marc Lammers
August 2009, one year after winning Olympic gold

1
Yes, a crisis!

It sounds weird, of course: coming second on the biggest sporting stage in the world and still feeling so low. That was when I realised that I would have to improve myself: I had to start with myself, not with the players. I was too much of a know-all. I had played hockey myself and taken the CIOS coaching course, so I reckoned I knew what it was all about. And then I realised that I didn't know it all. From that moment on, I started taking all sorts of courses. I started teaching myself and I went on work placements to learn. The crisis after the 2004 Olympics in Athens did improve me, in the long term. Otherwise I would have continued along the same path. Yet we had another deep crisis shortly before the Games in China: the 2007 Euro Hockey Nations Championship in Manchester. Another final that we lost. I had to take action, because if you do whatever it was you did four years earlier again, the results will be the same too. But I wanted more. I wanted to win.

Dyslexia, drive, and the calm of a crisis

By 2004 I had been the national team's manager for four years. A nice length of time, four years, with a big collection of silver medals that included the Olympic one from Athens. There was also a lot of whingeing, lots of swearing, players who had very much had enough of it all. A lost final. National hockey association board members who were openly asking if I should stay in my post. A thorough investigation followed, speaking to the players and the supporting team. I could have made the decision myself and run. I could have stopped then, and the association would have been happy enough if I had. But I thought: no, I would keep going.

That also had a lot to do with my own past. I was diagnosed as dyslexic when I was 24. It had affected my childhood quite strongly. Dyslexia was not as socially accepted then as it is now. Nobody really knew what it was. The net result was that my school grades were poor. My teachers didn't see that as dyslexia, but translated it into 'Marc is lazy', 'Marc is idle' or worse, 'Marc is stupid.' I can still see my English teacher jumping up and down when I failed to understand something yet again. He had no idea. He kicked me out of the class. I went home in tears on my bike. I could forget the Sports Academy, my big dream. I ask my mother if I could please go to the CIOS (the *Central Institute for Training Sports Leaders*). A blessing. There, I suddenly turned out to be good at something. At teaching, for example. That English teacher has always been a driving force for me: I'll show you that I can handle it! The Olympic final that we lost in 2004 was the same. The easy way would have been to admit it. Accept the idea that I wasn't up to it. But I decided not to. Fight, keep going. But now? Continuing meant commitment to another cycle of four years. Throughout those four years, I had just one goal: to get from second place to first. To show everyone that I *was* up to it.

The newspaper articles from that period said, "Marc Lammers is a very good trainer and coach, but without killer instinct. He'll always come second."
That was one of the things that motivated me to continue. Believe me, the period after the Olympics was more than just a dip for me. Ask my wife. She thought I was never going to pull myself out of it. Playing hockey and coaching were the only things I could do. And I was at a point where I thought I could not go on. What do you do then? I started thinking that second place was where I belonged. Second at the European Championships, second at the World Cup, second in the Champions Trophy, second at the Olympic Games. But that English teacher still haunted me. I had to show him that I was up to it.

I knew that I also had to change myself. I had become too much of a manager, whereas I am naturally full of passion, energy, conviction. And intuition too. I went back to square one. I started teaching myself, through work placements and courses. And I started paying more attention to the training sessions with the Dutch team. So, as part of the preparations for Beijing, I pushed myself back more into the role of trainer. Demonstrating the exercises myself more. Actually being on the pitch with a stick in my hands. I repositioned myself closer to the team. Everyone has their own core qualities. It would be unfair to tell the girls they had to make more of their core qualities if I wasn't making the most of my own. So I went back onto the pitch, among the players, talking and gesticulating, larking about or swearing. Until then, the matches and the results had been the top priority. But just playing matches won't make you any better, because a match can only be played using the skills you have already mastered. We were ranked three in the world in 2000; I wanted to be number one. By 2004 we were second, so we weren't there yet. And so there was no way to avoid more training.

In the business world you generally have next to no time for training. Every mistake is punished. But there are opportunities during a crisis. Get people to change places, even if only temporarily. Let them see what the others are doing; get them to learn from each other. You can bet that they will come up with new ideas.

Not so long ago, I was talking to a businessman in the clothing sector. His business consists of buying the right clothes and then selling those clothes on to shops. The sales staff always found something to comment on about the purchases: "How on earth could they have bought this shade of green? I'll never sell that!"
And the purchasers were always grumbling about the 'spoilt' sales staff in their flash company cars. This particular entrepreneur decided to send his purchasers on the road with the sales team for a day or so. And the sales staff were allowed to go along to a show in Italy to choose the new colours.

The buyers had to be there by six thirty in the morning ("But you don't have to be at the customer's till nine, surely?") and they had no idea of the traffic problems that the sales staff encountered every day. The sales team had to work their way through ten exhibition halls, without even a cup of coffee ("You have a great time there in Italy, drinking the bubbly all day..."). If this businessman had not had a crisis, he would never have been able to train his team in this way. There are often disagreements between purchasing and sales in a commercial organisation. Generally not just because their objectives are different, but because their value systems for those objectives are different. The purchasing team are defenders: they work together, they communicate, act collectively. Sales staff are attackers: it's about scoring, passion, freedom. If you put the two together and then get them both to put together a list of priorities for the company's values, you can get a very interesting discussion. And they will recognize and acknowledge the differences.

Opportunity 1: Cherish the calm that a crisis creates

Companies who have less work on their hands during a crisis should actually be pleased. They are being given time to make improvements. Over recent years, these companies will have only been 'playing competitive matches'. Only doing what they were good at; after all, every match has to be won. Thinking outside the box in particular was seen as a waste of time. Gain territory and keep pushing forward. A crisis offers you a chance to change course. An economic crisis is a quieter period for many companies and organisations. Cherish that calm: at last there is time to think about tomorrow. The customers won't be lining up today anyway.

Image rights, babes and an Olympic pilot light

I wanted to change a number of things in the team after we lost the final of the 2007 European Championships in Manchester. The way we played, the players, all sorts of things. I ought to have set that in motion a year earlier, but then we became world champions in Madrid.

I knew even then that some things would have to change, though. But all people ever said to me was, “Why? Isn’t it okay as it is?”
The Europeans in Manchester actually went pretty well until the final. If you look at the results, anyway. The process, the way we played there, was downright poor. We played the final against Germany and we lost. The ultimate confirmation for me that it really wasn’t quite right yet. The laziness, the (often unvoiced) irritations. One group wanted to eat in the hotel, the others wanted to go out with their boyfriends for once. More discipline, less discipline. Things weren’t quite right, we weren’t clicking and we all knew it one way or another. There was no hierarchy. Minke Booij and Fatima Moreira de Melo were the leaders in the team. But Minke was busy with all sorts of presentations and Fatima kept having photo shoots during the training sessions for the Rabobank advertising campaign. Everyone was busy, but with the wrong things. Even the manager wasn’t fully focused. I had been riding the crest of the wave too, after the gold at the World Cup. I was busy with presentations and lectures too.

On top of that, there was a lot of fuss at the time about the players’ image rights. Strangely enough, these were owned by the hockey association, although that was not legally possible. The players were busy getting that sorted, because – just like the association – they wanted to reap the commercial benefits of their fame as national team members. The association only owned the image rights of the team as a whole; the individual image rights belonged to the players. However, the rights were important for the association for bringing in sponsorship, which in turn allowed the team to travel around the globe. An affair that had nothing to do with the actual hockey, but showed the unhealthy atmosphere that had crept into the team. And I was in the middle of it all, employed by the hockey association but able to understand the players’ point of view. And the girls took all this bag-

gage with them to the training sessions and the matches. The lawyer that the players had brought in produced a website that went live the day before the first match of the European Championships. It stated that the players were going to sell their image rights individually.
Very possibly to the ABN-AMRO bank, a competitor of the main sponsor of the association, the Rabobank. The whole hockey association was in turmoil. The first day of the Europeans... The chairman rang me to ask what we thought we were up to. Crisis, in spades. I arranged a meeting with Minke and Fatima and asked what was going on and why they had set up a website like that. The girls were shocked by the question. "Oh, no!" They didn't know either that their lawyer had set the ball rolling. The players had not given instructions for that at all. So a couple of hours before our first match, I was still arranging for the website to be taken offline. It was only months after the Europeans, in Oman in November 2007, that I heard that I didn't have to worry any more and that the image rights affair had all been settled.

On top of all that, the documentary film *Goud* (Gold) was in the cinemas in the months leading up to the Euro Hockey Nations Championship in Manchester. It was a documentary that had been made during the preparations for the World Cup in Madrid in 2006, which we had won. The Dutch hockey team had been followed by a camera team for ten months, and nine hundred hours of pictures had then been reduced to a ninety-minute film. I still think that the film gives a distorted view of what we did. Much too much blubbing, as if the girls had been bursting into tears every day. However, the cinema audiences very clearly disagreed with me. The red carpet was out everywhere. Minke and Fatima were the players who were most in demand for premieres, interviews and so forth. Those two were so busy that they were left simply unable to do the work during training. Normally those two led from the front at training sessions, but now they weren't even able to join in. We had not made proper agreements about all this amongst ourselves and within the team. That was my fault too; it was my responsibility. We had done that before the Worlds in Madrid: we always asked each other beforehand what we wanted. That's an easy one: we want to win. The team also always said that winning is more important than taking part.

We also always agreed on the values that we wanted to express as a team. I let them make their own minds up about that generally, but not just before the Europeans. I was one of the people who thought it was all stumbling along nicely and I hadn't responded sharply enough. But that was why we all got so niggly during those European Championships. Misunderstandings about agreements, the food at the hotel wasn't right, whether or not to train every day... It all became a house of cards.

It is only when you look back at the crisis of those championships that you see that losing the final, which confirmed there were things wrong with the process, showed that there was a crisis. If you are still in the process and winning, you think that can't be all that bad. That is the amazing thing about a crisis. You know it's there, but you think you will get away with it. Discovering that your premonition was right makes it twice as hard to take. And then you say that you didn't see it coming. But you know you did.

In the financial world too, they saw something was coming. Confidence was sky-high, and so were the bonuses. Everything was going too well and the bankers thought they would get away with it. Shareholders had lost the picture too. It was like the *hockey babes* of the Dutch team. "We'll win anyway – we're that good."
Our European Championships crisis lasted months. During that period, everyone also had their own way of dealing with it. Some kept quiet and thought it would all blow over as the 2008 Olympics approached. Others were in an absolute panic and started telling the hockey association everything that was wrong. They kept me out of the loop too. Some said that losing the final had just been bad luck. But I knew straight away that it wasn't. Everyone dealt with the crisis differently. Until we went off to-

gether to make a plan, away from the familiar surroundings, looking for new ideas and insight. All singing from the same hymn sheet. And with our eye on the ball. It may not have been an Olympic flame yet, but at least the pilot light was on.

The map, the values, and us sitting in the sand
Several important players were also injured at the end of 2007. Minke Booij, Fatima Moreira de Melo, Miek van Geenhuizen and Kim Lammers. Maartje Paumen had torn a medial cruciate ligament in the 2007 European semi-final. Our penalty corner specialist was out of the final; we got ten short corners and didn't score a single one. We were afraid Maartje might not make the Olympics in China.

I was very worried. I though that we had learned from losing the final of the European Championships. I had even taken the blame in full for the short corner we missed in the final that caused our defeat; Germany scored on the counter from the missed penalty corner. I made my excuses as the press conference: "My fault, a poor choice, I'm sorry" – even before the first question had been asked. That press conference only lasted a couple of minutes.
That took the heat of the players and the discussions in the media soon died down. "It was the manager's fault." The players appreciated that, because they knew better.

If you are responsible for a team and you are in trouble, make sure you shoulder the blame too. When managers and directors start twisting and turning, the effect is negative. Admit your mistakes, even if you know you're not the only one to blame. That relieves the pressure and lets the team feel they can trust you and that you're there for them when you're needed.

I hoped that my confession would calm things down within the team, and more particularly allow them to focus on the next challenge: China. The picture was still fuzzy, though by now it was October 2007. Irritations among the coaching staff. Lots of excuses. Winners have plans; losers have excuses. So there was only one thing for it: if we wanted to win again, we needed a plan.

But how can you produce a plan for a team that can no longer work together? You have to go back to basics, together.

Not on a hockey tour this time, or a training camp with practice games against other top teams. No, something completely different. I had already discussed it earlier with our coaching staff's sports psychologist, Rico Schuijers. I also wanted him to come along if we chose a different destination this time. We went to Oman, a desert country bordering Saudi Arabia. Brigitte van de Tuin, my secretary at the national association, had lived there. She advised me to go there if I wanted to get right away from it all with the team. Off to the desert.

We had convinced the hockey association to try this approach by agreeing a practice match against Australia in Oman. You don't play them so often, because of the distances involved. Oman is about halfway between the Netherlands and Australia. But just after we had booked the whole trip, Australia pulled out... which wasn't actually a bad thing. It meant that we could focus fully on the team, on ourselves. At Schiphol airport, I said to Rico and my assistants, "I think that the next two weeks are crucial to our preparations for the Olympics in China. These are going to be the two key weeks of the whole eight years, because we can forget the Olympics if this doesn't resolve anything."
At the time, I really didn't think we would manage it. I was very unsure, not convinced it would work out right.

I did not have a plan. That was the main cause of all the trouble after the European Championships. Everyone was arguing with somebody else; we were busy doing the wrong things. You can often tell there are problems in a women's team because they stop talking to each other and start talking *about* each other. I no longer believed in it; I was right up shit creek. So far up it that I had wanted to ask the girls if they wouldn't prefer to move on with another manager. I was really insecure. Then the sports psychologist said to me, "Marc, you'll only know that in two weeks' time. You'll see things clearly again when we get back from Oman."

Oman really was back to basics. Off you go to an Arabian sandpit. We had invited India and Azerbaijan as opponents for a couple of friendlies. So that we could at least play the odd game, despite Australia calling it off. But it was soon not about hockey at all. We went into the desert together for three days. We slept in a tented camp for two nights, and that was where things turned around. We were right in the back of beyond, miles away from any luxury. Desert sand between your buttocks, a straw mattress, extreme heat during the day and icy cold at night. The girls were shivering in their beds, it was that cold. We spent most of the night round a big camp fire, simply for the warmth. Singing, together. Taking turns to sing a song. And then they started talking.

That first evening, I didn't twig what was happening at all. I was annoyed by the fact that the girls weren't asleep yet and I complained that they would catch colds; I was still caught in the treadmill of having to perform. Looking back, I can see what an idiot I had been. For not seeing it straight away. In fact, that camp fire was also what started calming me down. I saw it for what it was the next evening and recognised the team spirit I was looking for. For the first time, there was a moment when I thought that it might all work out right after all. There we were, all of us, staring into that fire. The Olympic flame? *The road to f(l)ame?*

After those days in the desert, we went back to the hotel. We had planned a number of sessions there with our sports psychologist for just the players. The team values resurfaced: what is important to us? What to we want to express? What are we prepared to do to achieve our goals? I was still unsure what the result would be. The only people I could talk to were Sandra le Poole and Rico Schuijers, our team manager and the sports psychologist, because both my assistants were in the same position as I was.

So I kept asking Sandra and Rico, "And now? So? What did the girls say? How is it going? Any progress? What are they talking about?"
In the end, those sessions were extremely important for the start of our preparations for the Olympic Games.

Those sessions produced a long list of no less than twenty 'team values'. The younger ones said that 'fun' was very important to them. The more senior ones mentioned 'fanaticism', 'focus' and 'fitness'. Then Rico told them "Now put them in order and give me the top four." Top of the list was 'commitment'. For example, sticking to agreements.
Number two was 'focus': having such a good picture of the processes, even the mental ones, that we know them better than all our opponents. We had to concentrate on the aspects that we could influence. The hockey itself, of course, but also everything associated with it.
Third was 'fitness': being in peak condition and showing it, with a visible determination to win. Everyone wanted to set personal bests in 'fitness' for China. To be fitter than ever before.
The fourth one was a typical women's one: it had to be fun, they had to enjoy themselves and they had to 'look good'. That one wouldn't have been on my list, but there you are...
Then Rico asked what standards the players would want to link to those values. After all, the standards provide the framework for the values. Commitment? Keeping your promises and training nine times a week. Monday, Tuesday and Wednesday were 'internal'. Training, resting, eating, sleeping. Working towards optimum fitness. At the end we came back to their final value, 'looking good'. The players said, "We want really nice kit for the Olympics, nice tight lines. We have to look happy, sign autographs for children and enjoy being with each other."
Suddenly I saw ambition in their eyes again. Energy. Passion. The whingeing stopped. Rico told me later that those three days in the desert had been where it turned around. "That camp fire. That really was the moment."

If you ask people after the event how the Dutch team appeared at the Beijing Olympics, then you will often hear those four values mentioned, even though we never revealed them.

> ***Opportunity 2: Get off the beaten track***
>
> *A crisis requires new insights. And you will not get those from the same old surroundings. Step outside your own biotope. We could have gone on a training tour to Argentina. We had done that often enough. We would undoubtedly have trained hard there. But in Oman, our ideas changed and we created the basis for a team of champions. In the desert sand.*

Then you see that the values you agree upon and adopt in your organisation can also be recognised by the outside world. But don't impose them from above! Many companies define their own values and implement them by imposing them on the staff. And that's where the trouble starts. You hear the management in the boardroom saying, "They aren't keeping their promises!" Hold on a moment – they didn't make that promise, the management imposed it on them!

We had not stated what our values were before the 2007 European Championships in Manchester. The result was that everyone kept looking at me if something didn't go well. I was a kind of policeman. Now that we had stated our values for the preparations for the 2008 Olympics, the players could correct one another. I was no longer the policeman, because everybody knew what the rules were. The sports psychologist also asked the players what they would do if someone failed to keep to those values. The girls said that they would tackle each other about it. The coach would only have to get involved in very exceptional or difficult issues. That was just how I wanted it. Three days in the desert yielded the desired result. Players who managed themselves, shouldering their responsibility.

2
China crisis

We went to the Olympic Games in Beijing and we were only allowed to take sixteen players instead of eighteen. Crisis! Every national team had to 'fire' two players! And it was for China, where the conditions were so tough. Disgraceful! But I thought: yes, the average level of the squad will be better than with eighteen. And there was no need for a benchmark against our competitors. After all, they were in the same boat. They had to drop people too. So it was no time to start hiding behind excuses.
Selecting the players who finally made the trip was a tough process. If you had asked all the hockey buffs in the Netherlands to produce a list of sixteen names, the names would not have been those of the players whom I finally did take to China. I took Liedewij Welten and Eva de Goede along. Two girls who were then just seventeen. Everyone looked at them and said, "No experience – that's not right!" But I had learned from the past that diversity is needed to give the team strength. Diversity in terms of age too. You mustn't have players who are all the same age. Those youngsters went to the Olympics thinking, "I'll be able to go a couple more times, so why not this one too? Great, isn't it? Cool! I can be part of it. And oh, Nadal's there too – wow!"

That frivolous side, that naivety. It really gave us a lot of energy. The 'kids' were not generally the ones who were nervous at the Olympics. Rather, it was the ones in the middle. The more senior ones had doubts sometimes too, feeling the responsibility.

Like a number of other key players, Minke Booij had been injured for a long period while we were preparing for China. Unlike the rest of the team, Miek van Geenhuizen and Fatima Moreira de Melo also had to keep training hard for two more weeks to make up for time lost due to injuries. Both these players had had long-term injuries during the season. Fatima had not played for months. This was during the period that I had to make choices for Beijing. The players were both put out that I was unsure about them; they thought it was ridiculous. But I knew that I would not be able to take them to the Olympics if they did not get fitter quickly. Their anger made them both fight determinedly, working extremely hard and deserving their places in the final squad.

In the meantime, the team was playing well without these stalwarts. It was also comforting to the older players to some extent, seeing that the team could function without them. It was good for Minke to see that the team was not dependent on her. That kept her calm. The fear of blowing it was often what drove her. That anxiety was eliminated because other players proved capable of taking over her role. She knew that she would only have to shoulder the burden of responsibility again when she was fully fit. And when she was fit, I wanted to be able to tell her above all to start playing again like she used to – with an abundance of energy, but also with freedom. I've known her since she was 13, when I was the coach of her girls' team.

I sent her and all the other players individual letters. That was at the opening of the Olympic Games, two days before our first match. They were short letters, scribbled on hotel notepaper. For Minke Booij, I wrote: "Go back to being that cheerful girl with the red face and the pony tail, stopping the centre forward neatly, diving in for everything. Then we'll see what happens. Your mum is already proud of you." (I knew that her mother had died a number of years ago.)
Later she said to me, "That's the moment I knew that I just had to do what I was good at."

All the girls got a letter like that, each focusing on their own strengths and the reasons why I had selected them. For Naomi van As, I wrote, "Why do you think you are here now, in China? Because you're a star, someone who's going to go right to the top, leading from the front."

And she did. I had not prepared those notes. It was a spontaneous idea, the day before. I had once heard that Foppe de Haan had once done that when he was the manager of the Dutch Under-21 football team. And I knew from my own wife that women do like to receive a card. Add that to the fact that I'm badly dyslexic, and you will soon realise that one or two of the notes made them laugh a lot, even if it was only because of the spelling. But that makes it even more personal. We spent that evening as a group, watching the opening ceremony on the telly. When I handed them the notes, I had said that they should only read them later when they were alone in their rooms. Exciting! I'd actually quite like to know if any of the players kept those notes...

My players were not allowed to go to the opening ceremony of the Games. After the European Championships, it was stated that NOC*NSF, the Dutch Olympic Committee, had changed the rules for athletes who wanted to be part of the opening. Athletes who had a match the day after the opening were not allowed to take part in the ceremony. That had previously meant 24 hours, but it had now been changed to 48 hours. And we were playing our first match 45 hours after the opening. So no ceremony. "Ridiculous," said the players. "They're taking all the fun out of it."

Yup – another crisis. In the end we watched it on TV together in 'Holland House', our own living room in the Olympic Village. And no fuss. Except those notes, that is. One good result was that everyone was so curious about what would be in the note that all the players went to bed early.

If you look at what kind of a person I am, you will see that a lot of what I do is driven by intuition rather than logic. I love facts and statistics, but when the chips are down I trust my gut feeling.

I wanted to give the girls something extra, something individual. That's why I went and wrote those notes.
It is about creativity too, certainly in a crisis. You could have a tendency to focus above all on things that you have already done. I think that you have to go back to the roots of the things you are good at, but that you must then use that as the foundations for looking for something different. I took a good look at myself too after we lost the 2004 Olympic final in Athens. I thought, what do I really do well, as a coach? I'm good at video analyses and I'm good at getting my enthusiasm across. I give them energy; I never stand around at a training session with my hands in my pockets – I'm always active. That basis of analysis and fervour is what I returned to after 2004. I went back onto the pitch more often again, in amongst the players. And once back to those roots, I attempted to deploy my strengths differently – as with those notes.

Companies and organisations do often go back to basics in a crisis, but they then keep on doing what they had always done. It is precisely the right time to dare to be different, to dare to innovate, above all in your approach, the way you go about things, because you must not fiddle about with the basics too much in a crisis. If you express things differently, you can generate more empathy and more involvement. I always held a pep talk before an important game. But before the first match of the Olympic Games in Beijing, I let Al Pacino do the talking, in Oliver Stone's film *Any Given Sunday*.

Inches, Dutch weather and Peppe's sandwich
Shortly before our first match of the Olympics in China, we were for a moment threatening once again to shift the emphasis from the process to the result. I heard the players expressing their worries to each other. "We really have to win that first game, because my parents are only coming to China to watch us

for the second week. I mean, we surely won't have been knocked out already?
And then we'll get all that fuss with the media again – they'll go for us if things don't go well."

That didn't half scare me. They weren't just talking about the result, oh no: they were even talking about the consequences of the result. When we had just agreed to focus on the process, on the things that we could influence. If you start focusing on the consequences of the result, then performances will drop off and you'll be a long way from achieving any kind of *flow*. I thought, "This is going wrong. I won't get the players back into line and concentrating on the process." Then I picked up the DVD of *Any Given Sunday*. Al Pacino has the lead role, playing the coach of an American football team. There is a scene in the film where they are in the team's dressing room just before a key game. Al Pacino addresses his team, in a way that goes right to the marrow of your bones. That was the clip I showed the girls of the Dutch hockey team the day before their first Olympic match against South Africa. Al Pacino boomed through 'Holland House': *"...Either we fight together, or we die alone... We have to play this match and struggle, inch by inch..."*

We had to beat South Africa inch by inch. Concentrating on the process, on our actions. And not on results, let alone the consequences of the results. What do you reckon? The next day, the rain was bucketing down. But it didn't affect us. Fatima Moreira de Melo called the toss. She wasn't a leader, but I often let her do the toss because she always seemed to make something out of it. It was an absolute cloudburst. Before the toss, she shook the South African captain's hand and said, *"Nice weather, huh? Yeah, real Dutch weather..."*
With a broad smile. Things like that. The first inch had been won.

Opportunity 3: Focus on the process and not on the result

If the process is correct, the result will fall into place. It is very tempting, particularly during a period of crisis, to get fixated by results. That is pointless. The process contains your plan, your stats and your strategy. The result is on the scoreboard, and once it's there, it's too late to do anything about it.

When there's a recession, why not show Al Pacino to your staff and management teams? Pictures say a lot more than words. You can inspire people in ten minutes. No training session can beat that. You can alter people's mindset by talking to them, by pressing the right buttons. But do intervene at once if you see things are going wrong, and stay focused on the things that you can control. The most difficult part for the coach or manager is recognising the situation, because you are one of the team, of course. Incidentally, the fact that you can recognise that something is going wrong in the team is probably the reason why you are the leader of the team.

We won the first match against South Africa convincingly. But we didn't play nearly so well in the second game against South Korea. We played way below our best in that match, even though we did win 3-2. We went and sat down together and asked how that could happen. I spoke to two or three players directly, naming names. "What's up with you, then?"
At which the whole group broke down in tears, crying.
"It's all so tense."
"It scares me. I've been in the Dutch team for four or five years, and I thought all that tension would pass. But I'm afraid."
Once again, the thought patterns were looking at the consequences of the result. Once again, we had to go back to the process. Little by little, it seemed that this was becoming one of my daily tasks as the manager.

It later turned out that it had been a very important talk. The mere fact that the tensions had been shared with the rest of the team started to release those tensions. Precisely because there were all sorts of different character types within the team.

The older players asked, “Do you really think that we’re not afraid of losing? I’ve been in the team for nine years and this is my third Olympics, but I’ve never won gold. I want to come first too, for once."
The only two who weren’t scared were the two seventeen-year-olds. After the discussion, they said to my assistant, “What are they talking about? These are the Olympics – I mean, this is amazing! Surely you should be enjoying it?”

From experience, no matter how strange it may sound, I knew that the Olympic village would become a drag. We traipsed past the same serving bowls again every meal, and the girls began to complain about the food being “the same yet again.” Nutrition is very important, particularly during a tough tournament like that, and it is often undervalued. You notice for example that the players start eating less and less, while their efforts require more and more. That is why I tried to find a different way of drawing their attention to the fact. During the second week of the games, I showed the girls a clip of my daughter Peppe when she was just two. For seven minutes, she did her utmost to make clear to Daddy that there was no way she was going to eat that sandwich that was on her plate. We were able to laugh at it together. When it becomes a drag, you have to do something new and surprising to break the pattern. Those notes to the players were another novelty. The actual content was mostly stuff that I had already said to them loads of times. But now it was on paper. Different. Not the norm.

We also did things differently during the preparations, shortly before the Olympics. For a major tournament, we generally travel to the destination two to three weeks beforehand. We did the same now. At that point it was still wonderfully calm in the

Olympic village. Other teams were still elsewhere in hotels, saying to themselves, "We'll be in that village plenty long enough." We were able to use the training facilities to our hearts' content, we were often able to use the competition pitch because not many other teams were there yet, and we could take our time laying out our rooms as we wanted.

Then came the changes to the norm: when it started to get busy in the Olympic village, two weeks before the start of the Games, we left again! We disappeared to a resort not far from Beijing for four days. Travelling light with just a weekend bag. That's how you break the pattern when it becomes a drag, with an unusual action. The Dutch Olympic Committee thought it was strange, but they are very focused on sportsmen and sportswomen as individuals. Going away for a week like that would indeed be killing for an athlete. But for a team like us, it was very good. We put a lot of training work in at that resort. A lot of it was on the tennis court! Exercises that were fun, but very tough. When we got back, we were absolutely ready for the tournament – we went to our rooms, we came 'home'. We had no need to train on the number one pitch any more, because we knew it like the back of our hand. If you look at all the teams, we are the one that trained most on pitch number one. That is extremely important for Maartje Paumen, our short corner specialist, because every circle is different. Thanks to the calm of that first week and the almost unlimited time that she was able to train on pitch 1, her confidence grew hugely. I had said to the keeper that she should let the first three shots in, so now the goalie said to Maartje, "Wow, what was that? Those were really travelling! Much faster than in Holland!"
This let Maartje Paumen really build up her confidence. But that could have affected the confidence of the keeper, Lisanne de Roever. I didn't want that. So on the next day, I asked the second short corner taker, Eva de Goede, not to hit the first few shots too hard. And that got Lisanne De Roever's self-confidence back. She stopped them all...

All in all, we did the opposite of the other teams. And they arrived, started training like mad, and then began taking it easier as the first match approached and the availability of the training facilities reduced.

After we came back to Beijing, after the resort, we kept on training flat out, both on and off the pitch. Nobody dared to follow that approach.

Jos Geijsel, the exercise physiologist, had decided that we could keep training hard throughout the tournament. This is known as *tapering on*, rather than *tapering off* (the usual method, in which you gradually reduce the intensity). We actually increased the intensity as the final came closer. This was a new approach in the world of team sports. That also meant it was difficult to convince everybody. The girls' parents, who then start saying, "This is all too much for my daughter." Sometimes I would think that maybe they were the ones for whom it was all too much, with all that fuss about their child... The situation in a team sport is very different than for individual athletes.
I mean, when we were kids we would all play football for three hours or more at a stretch in the street, wouldn't we? And there wasn't a coach next to you then yelling, "Watch out, you'll overdo it!" It is something that I see increasingly often, the cotton wool approach to youngsters. No cost and no effort are too great, physiotherapists are involved... you name it. I can tell you for a fact that my team had more injuries if there was a physio present. If there wasn't one, then there were no injuries... Ultimately, the players have to do it themselves. My job as a manager is to create the conditions that will allow them to perform at their best. That is why we went to that resort, why we built up the confidence and why we increased the level of the training, with shorter but more intense sessions. At the same level as a match. Half the players thought it was ridiculous. They compared it with the opposition, who were lying by the pool. Except for the Chinese, that is, who were training for four hours a day in the sweltering heat. We met in the final – the only two teams who had also trained on the rest days...

An overload is just doing that little bit more than the system can handle. Over-training is almost impossible in a dynamic sport like hockey. I sometimes heard parents or club trainers say, "She is over-trained." That's not true; the girl is just mentally fatigued. She had made a few wrong choices that week – come to a party, stayed up too late studying, that sort of thing.

We were together nine times a week. The girls were playing the sport nine times a week. Overdoing the training? Then you would have to practise nine times a week at the very top competition level, but we never did that. There is no point to it anyway. It will not make you any better. During those nine times that we met up, we also had our discussions with the mental coaches, our sessions with the exercise physiologists and dieticians: everything that could affect performance. We trained four times a week for 20 minutes above the lactic acid threshold, 'in the red' as it were. If we had done that ten times a week for half an hour, then we would have become overloaded. But by then we would also have lost out in terms of quality in many other areas. In sports such as athletics and swimming, where times are crucial, it is possible to over-train. In team sports such as hockey, there is always compensation between your own efforts and the efforts of other team members. Fitness training alone will not win you any matches. Neither will training that is purely focused on technique. Look for the right balance, even in a crisis.

3

Always change a winning team

During a tournament, I always stuck to one team. But in between the big tournaments, I always let players go and added new players. Even if we won a tournament. My motto? Always change a winning team. We had won the 2006 World Cup in Madrid, so I could have left everything as it was. We were finalists at the Europeans in 2007, so why change things? Precisely because these are the right moments to act. To become an even better team. Are things running smoothly at the company? Fire a manager! You should see how hard the other managers work after that. The culture should focus on competitive effort. Getting better every day. 4-0 has to become 5-0. What you need are fighters. Tough characters can beat better players than themselves. You can influence the desired culture by your team selections.
How many times do we see company departments full of people who haven't had this sense of competition for a long time? They don't need to get better, they are contented enough. Things are very easy for a national team manager in such a case: you just drop a player like that from the team. Things are a bit more difficult for an entrepreneur or company director, but that should not stop them from considering it, to say the least. Just do it. Saying goodbye costs money at that particular moment, but in the long run it will yield money. Just work it out after five years.

Australia, for instance, has relatively flexible laws about terminating employment. The first year after this new law about termination of employment was implemented, unemployment rose. But so did the results of companies.

The years after that unemployment rates were historically low, while the results of companies remained positive. It took five years before things were okay again, but currently everyone is benefiting from it. My prediction is that the Netherlands will have to deal with it sooner or later too.

Setting up a team is a difficult job. What do we often do, even in business circles? We go looking for the same types. When I started working as a manager, I was only looking for Marc Lammers types. "That will make me world champion..." Later on I thought: "No, stupid, did you ever score back then? Nope. I never scored!"
Well, you'll never be world champion then. A team made up of the same type of player will never achieve the results achieved by a team of complementary types. Diversity is a necessary precondition for a good team, but not a sufficient condition. Real Madrid had been the team of the *galacticos*, the superstars, for years. The best players in the world, but never a tight-knit team.

As well as being diverse, the team members must also complement each other.

Let's assume that twenty employees have to be dismissed because of the crisis. As the director of the company, you're inclined to dismiss the people who you rarely have to deal with. But in fact, those may be the people who make sure that your team is balanced.

Even if I had the best 'conduits' and the best at robbing the ball in midfield and the best wingers waiting for the ball, that won't make me a world champion. The challenge is to get those three playing together. Diversity is therefore the strength of your team, as long as they're willing to cooperate. A team is complementary, if the strengths of team members compensate the weaknesses of others.

I'm sure that the executive boards of banks would have made other decisions, prior to the credit crisis, if there had been more women in them.

Women would consider customer care much earlier on, rather than bonuses or shareholders. They would avoid risks much more, as they don't want to run risks with money that belongs to other people, the customers. Men are tough guys; they want more, more and more. This is also in the interest of the ever-demanding shareholders.
On the other hand, women communicate in a typically feminine way. If things are okay, they talk *to* each other. But if things are not okay, they talk *about* each other. I was the assistant to Tom van 't Hek, the national team manager in 2000. He said, "Women are like a heathland fire. If you see any smoke, put out the fire at once. If you wait a bit too long, the whole moor will be ablaze!" Men think much more of the content, say what they have to say and continue after that. They don't mind saying to each other, "You shouldn't have done that, shithead. If you do that again, I'll knock your block off! Right, fancy another beer?"

In my experience, you can convince men using the content and women using emotions. Women are much more disciplined. They are much more loyal to each other, much more used to achieving things together. Men prefer to do things on their own and they are quicker to tell you that they can do something when they can't. Women on the other hand, say that they can't do it when they actually can. You have to support women much more often too in a positive way and show understanding. Men need to be slowed down to prevent them from becoming arrogant. Just an example: when I say to the girls, "Come on, ladies, time for a run anticlockwise round the pitch," they start jogging before I have finished. Men won't do that. They would say: "Anticlockwise? Why not right-handed?" You have to use the content to convince them. They will only do it if you can convince them. Incidentally, the women will do it but you may well hear them whispering on the way. "Ridiculous, don't you think? Insisting on going anticlockwise..." This is how they avoid the conflict with their coach. They prefer to talk about it with their friends. Men quarrel functionally, based on content.

As the national team manager, I had to deal not only with my team members, but also with my 'shareholders'. On the one hand there was the hockey association, on the other the media. They are always breathing down your neck, telling you over and over again that you have to win. We went to the Champions Trophy in 2008 with what the media said was a B-team. It was a deliberate choice on my part. The playoffs in the Dutch competition were still being held. I wanted to try out a few younger players and I wanted to encourage the discussion about the restriction to sixteen players for the Olympics.
Only sixteen players would be allowed to go the Olympic Games, two fewer than to the World Cup or the Champions Trophy. I said straight away, "Okay, but in that case I'll take only one goalie along." The entire international hockey world though I was just trying to provoke a reaction. But I really meant it.
The international hockey association FIH thought that it would all blow over. Other managers had also said that they would take the one goalie with them. But I was the only manager who actually did it, at the 2008 Champions Trophy in Germany. Eighteen players were allowed to go, but I still took only one goalie with me. Firstly because I didn't want to give in and to show the FIH that I really meant it. And secondly to see how the team would respond to having just one keeper in the group. How would they deal with it during the matches and during the training sessions? And thirdly, I wanted to gain experience with having just one goalie at a big tournament, as a preparation for my plans for the Beijing Olympic Games.

I would be running the risk of my keeper getting injured, but in exchange for that I was able to take one extra outfield player along. In view of the extreme circumstances that we would be facing in China, this was a much more valuable option for me.

And anyway, goalies hardly ever get injured during matches; if they get injured at all, it's usually in training sessions. So we made changes to the practice sessions to protect our keeper.

Eventually, this cry for help ensured that we were able to take two additional players to China as reserves who would be called in if a player got hurt during the tournament. Despite the potential risk of giving in, the FIH did concede, as I was able to make my motives clear to them through my actions at the Champions Trophy.

So I did take just one goalkeeper with me, both to the Champions Trophy in 2008 and the Olympics in 2008. In China there was a second goalie on standby, who could be called in if the first girl picked up an injury. The risk of having only one keeper in the squad was then reduced to not being able to replace the goalie during the match. I took that risk consciously.

What did we gain from that during the Olympic Games? We could play our matches in perfect confidence with just one keeper (we had done that before at a big tournament). And we benefited from the additional rest for all the other team members afforded by the additional player; the extra players made it possible to substitute players more often and rest them more.
Our main competitors Argentina (semi-final) and China (final) hadn‘t dared to do this and so they had a reserve goalie on the bench who didn't play at all. They didn't have the extra option of changing field players that I had. It was another gain of two per cent over my competitors. At the very least...

Innovations, ice baths and competitors
You can't play hockey in China. The heat was a crisis, and so were the humidity and the smog. In fact, it was virtually irresponsible to hold a sports tournament under such conditions. But what applied to us, applied to our opponents as well.
What is important in a crisis situation is not how well you deal with it, but how well you are doing in comparison to your com-

petitors. We therefore had to learn to cope with the heat, humidity and smog better than they did. Yes I know, they call me the innovator of the hockey world, but don't be mistaken – most of the innovations don't work.

And that applies to me too. But it's about the innovations that do work. If there are three of those, whereas my opponents do not introduce anything new, then I've made a tidy profit.

What we did in the very first place was to regulate the pulse of the players who were being substituted. We used ice jackets. In hockey, the manager is allowed to substitute players at will during the match. I made ample use of this option for the forwards in particular; I also let them each play exactly the same amount of time. They sat down on the bench, tired and with a high pulse rate. But they couldn't get rid of their body heat because of the ambient temperatures. That's when we decided to work with ice jackets to cool the body down faster during the match. An idea that I had borrowed from the military. The soldiers had to overcome the same problem during their missions in Iraq. When I visited a barracks, I was shown how to use with cooling jackets and cooling collars. Months later – while on another training secondment – I visited Anky van Grunsven, triple Olympic gold medallist in dressage. My wife and children enjoyed the horses and I saw ice jackets there too. Ice jackets for horses have been used for a very long time now in equestrian sports. Not that I'm calling my players were horses... I thought it was a great idea and with the help of TNO we developed ice jackets for the team members. Another nice example of thinking outside the box. When I look at my own sport, I can only see the problems. When I look around in other sports, I suddenly see alternatives.

We also experimented with oxygen masks as a weapon against the smog. Fresh oxygen lets you recover quickly. We didn't use it in the end, though. In addition, transpiration was a problem; some players lost up to four litres of fluid during a match. Try to

replenish that in just a few hours... We even considered using infusions. But we didn't do that either. But they were all innovations that we thought about for four years. Investigations, doctors, TNO, DSM.
Two months before the tournament, it was announced during a medical meeting of the IOC that drips and oxygen were not allowed, except for emergencies.
But on the other hand, what's an emergency? NOC*NSF left me to decide on that one. In the end, I didn't dare to take the risk. So as you can see, a lot of innovations fail too.

We kept statistics on the body temperatures and pulse rates of all the players. We had been in China before, so we knew what to expect. If you stood there on the artificial grass in August in the middle of the day, it could be 45°C on the pitch! The average body temperature of the players during the match was 40°C. The goalie's temperature even went up to 41°C, which is a high fever. Their pulse rates were still up at 150 a minute an hour after the match.
That was when I thought, "Hey, an opportunity. If we can accelerate that fatigue recovery process, we can create a lead over our competitors." Cooling jackets had been discovered in the equestrian world and were widely used; these jackets were then 'reinvented' for the Dutch hockey players.

The second innovation that we implemented was ice baths. That one got us onto TV and it was in all the papers. After the match our players sat in tubs or children's baths filled with ice-cold water. It seemed a rather Spartan approach, but we developed it into a very nifty system. The time and temperature were carefully dosed, matched to the individual players' needs. We started using them at the 2006 World Cup. All the teething problems had been ironed out before the Games in 2008.
A lot of people must have looked perplexed as wheelbarrows full of ice were taken to our dressing room. You could almost hear people thinking, "Wow, they must have a lot of injuries."

Our opponents saw that too and soon worked out that we were using ice baths to accelerate muscle and body temperature recovery times.

So other countries began to copy us. And that's where innovations can go wrong: you shouldn't imitate others slavishly, because you'll copy the teething problems too. But in this case I didn't mind. More than that: I had the story of the ice baths spread around by a team member. I said to her, "Tell the foreign girls in your club team, just as a joke of course, that I get you to sit in water at 5 °C for twenty minutes." There were two foreign girls, players with one of our competitors, in her club team.

And so that national team started to use ice baths too. The coach thought, "The Dutch have studied this a lot more than we have." In fact, those studies had shown that customised ice baths should be used. First a bath at 12°C after a match. Next a 6°C ice bath for five minutes for the smaller, thinner players. The larger players sat in that for seven minutes and the biggest players for ten minutes. You recover more quickly if you cool down fast, but cooling down too quickly is bad for the muscles. In addition, your body reacts by shivering in order to make as many muscles as possible work in order to generate heat. Using the ice baths wrongly will therefore work out wrong.

During the Games we saw the players of that other national team wearing thick shawls at dinner, shivering with cold. They failed to match the treatment to the individual team members' physiques; they just sat down in ice baths for 15 minutes. So be glad if your competitor copies you! They don't know what you know. Let them do whatever they want to do. From that moment on, you will still be benefiting from your own innovation while your opponent is tackling the problems with it. And you can keep blithely working on your next innovation.

Your competitor is racked by doubts, precisely because he has copied the teething troubles as well. "See, it doesn't work!" and then everything reverts to the old situation and your innovation is no longer considered.

Eventually the other team in question decided not to use the baths any more.

During the Olympics, only Australia was using them. But a different problem had to be dealt with that we had already discovered in China a year before. Tap water in China can be 28°C, much warmer than in the Netherlands. So the three hundred kilos of ice that we needed after the match melted in no time. In fact, we needed eight hundred kilos of ice. I knew that it would be impossible for us to get hold of that during the Olympics. Together with DSM, we developed a cooling machine. A box measuring one and a half metres in length and width that could turning water at 28°C into water at 6°C in just a few minutes. But you should have seen us trying to get that machine on wheels past security to the pitch or the dressing room. Innovation can be hard work... NOC*NSF thought it was all ridiculous. What a fuss, sort it out yourself. The machine had to go through the scanners, with the police looking on. Eventually the box got through. We were the only country that could use it. Australia couldn't. Our players had recovered reasonably well just fifteen minutes after the match. We tried to simulate the intensity of the matches at the training sessions too, and so the girls had to hop into those ice baths after practising too. You should have seen our opponents' faces.

The flip side of innovations is that you may depend on them too much. The team were against it at first. "I'm not going to sit in that stupid little bath! Four years ago we were second and we got hot showers! Who's telling me that we'll be first if we use those baths?" There was a lot of resistance among the team members. Whereas I had initially had to fight people from the hockey association in particular, I had to focus on the players themselves now. After the World Cup in 2006 they said, "Marc, this was great, we're world champions. No more changes now, please. Don't make any changes, leave everything as it is!"

But I knew that we had to keep making changes. Conditions in Beijing were quite different from Madrid. I managed to convince them about the baths, about this innovation. But then they depended on it too much. "Oh, I hope we've got ice baths! Otherwise I won't recover properly..."

Another thing to cope with. So if the customs officer in Beijing had said that we were not allowed to take our 'cooling machine' with us, I would have been in a lot of trouble. But think of what Philips' business policy used to be: at least ten innovations every year. You'll always have one or two that can be applied. Don't depend too much on any single innovation. And sometimes the things that you don't have high expectations of can turn out to be the most successful.

Opportunity 4: Compare your achievements against your competitors

When you're in a crisis, there's no point comparing results with the situation before the crisis. Companies whose turnover decreases by 25% in a crisis might feel that they're doing very badly. But that isn't the case if their competitors' turnover has dropped by 40%. To become a champion, you need only to do one thing: keep winning the next match by beating the next opponent. That'll make the crisis seem much simpler.

Ethical boundaries, deaf players, and 'leaking baths'

Our baths and jackets were in no way a distortion of the competition. Other countries could have done it too. Here's a different example: I also considered using intravenous drips, to replenish the fluid that players lost during the match faster. But that takes you into the field of ethics. Is this acceptable? Where's my limit? Well, if we have to use needles, I don't want to be part of it. After all, it is perfectly possible to administer nutrients or medication by that route too. As far as I'm concerned, it's getting too close to cycle racing. And what about unfair competition? Let me tell you a secret... The goal posts of a hockey goal used to be a bit flexible and just loose on the pitch. So a couple of our players would kick the posts of our own goal inwards a couple of times, making sure that the posts were a little closer together. Just a few centimetres... And on the other side, if they could get there, they would knock those posts a little bit outwards. During an important match for the Champions Trophy in 2002, a ball hit our post when the scores were tied.

"Just as well we shifted that post a little bit inwards, isn't it, Marc?" they said to me. Well, was that ethically responsible? Is it allowable? Later on hockey goals were fixed into the ground, so it's no longer possible. But it's the referee's job to make sure that the goals are placed exactly right, isn't it?

Innovations do not only let you accelerate your own processes and development. You can also slow down your competitor's processes. Leaking the information about the use of ice baths to competitors is just such an example.

But we did the same with the use of 'ear-pieces' during the 2006 World Cup. We made better use of our own penalty corners and misled our opponents. How did it work? I had been invited by the Rabobank to join them in the Tour de France for a day in 2004. Sitting on the back seat of the team leader's car, it was where I saw 'ear-pieces' being used for the first time, a link between the team leader and his cyclists, who wore small earphones. I thought it was fantastic and immediately saw opportunities for the hockey team.

Wouldn't it be ideal it if I could be connected directly with my team members, without other people hearing what I was saying! I called my wife from the Tour de France and asked her to check the hockey regulations and see if they said anything about telecommunication. The rules did not prohibit it. Going onto the pitch with any device that might hurt other players was banned, though. So the box, that little transmitter that the cyclists used, had to be modified. TNO introduced me to a company called Phonac. They knew what they were about and a few weeks later those transmitters were in the back of my car. The girls wouldn't

be very pleased at first, I knew that. "Oh, it's an innovation, is it?"
So I introduced it as a joke to start with. "Let's try it out once and have a bit of fun," I said to Mijntje Donners. That got the group's resident hard case in on my plan. We tested it. It was a tiny little transmitter, stuck to her ear with a piece of sticking plaster.

We got a penalty corner in a match and I used gestures to signal which corner I wanted. But in Mijntje's ear I asked for another variant. Mijntje passed it on to her team members but they were worried that I would get angry. "Trust me," said Mijntje. We scored from that corner. Of course, after the match the players were afraid I was going to be cross. They thought that they had not stuck to the agreements. After the match, I did ask (hiding a smile) what the hell they thought they had been playing at with that last corner. Shocked, the girls pointed at Mijntje. That was when I told them that I had whispered to Mijntje which corner I really wanted. "Hey, what have you got in your ear?" they asked Mijntje. And from that moment on, it was accepted by everyone. It was our company secret. It gave me the option of telling the players concerned which short corner variant to use. But not much more, because they immediately told me that they didn't want me barking orders in their ears all match.

In the years before that, the famous 'video goggles' had already given me the ability to see the opponent's defenders in 3D when we were taking short corners. Just a single corner was enough for me to see how the defenders ran out and where the gaps for scoring were. A simple signal to the girls taking the short corners was enough to get the goals rolling in. But that simple signal got more difficult in the years that followed. Opponents could hear and see my signals too and were able to adapt their defences again. I switched to baseball signals. It was a trick I had picked up from Robert Eenhorn, the national coach for the Dutch baseball team, who had told me about the secret hand signal codes used in that sport. You can see coaches tapping on their arms, then a tap against their cap, then a hand brushing down the upper arm. All very secret. But what happened? Opponents would video me during matches and analyse all those codes. So as soon as I gave a signal, the opponent often also knew which short corner was coming. Those ear-pieces opened up a whole new world for me.

So there I was by the touchline, signalling for all I was worth. And the opponents would watch carefully and work out the code too: penalty corner number eighteen, that's the double move passing it to the left for the flick shot. And in the meantime I would say to the players in their earpieces, "Listen girls, we're doing penalty corner number seven, off to the right..." Goal. Our innovation didn't just make our short corners better – it made the opposition defence worse!

The success of those earpieces began by winning Mijntje Donners over. She was one of the group's leaders, very experienced and highly critical. Once she was on my side, introducing an innovation to the team was a lot easier. What you often see in organisations is that the changes are carried through for the 'easy victims', newcomers or staff who do not have the respect of others. It puts pressure on that innovation. You're better off finding someone, no matter how tricky it may be to convince them, who will ensure that people trust the innovation when it is introduced, giving it backing and credibility.

The ear-pieces were banned too in the end. But they served us well at the World Cup in Perth in 2002. I can still remember a photographer from the Telegraaf paper coming up to me with a picture afterwards. "Tell me Marc, what's that? In that player's ear?" I was worried and asked him to keep it quiet. "Sure, I get the picture. A girl like that doesn't want everyone to know she's a bit deaf, of course... You won't hear me mentioning it." I nodded, thanking my lucky stars that he hadn't asked for the real reason. After the semifinal, which we won, he came up to me again. "Nice one, Marc, having a girl on your team with a hearing aid. But what's really going on? I mean, don't tell me there are eight deaf players. That's stretching it a bit..." So I told him. And a couple of months later there was a new rule that banned the use of telecommunications with the players from then on. But we had still got second place at the 2002 World Cup!

You shouldn't make such a big thing of it anyway. Even with an ear-piece, you still have to get the ball into the net.

Whether you win or lose, innovation costs nothing

It's right that they were banned in the end. The ear-piece went a bit against my principles too. I like it if the players make their own decisions, think about things and understand what's happening during a match. At key moments, I was starting to tell them what they had to do. And so there are innovations that can help you out of a crisis, but need to be ditched again afterwards. The end justifies the means, but not for all time. Let's have a think about vision when taking a corner. It's very awkward for the player who is shooting or pushing to keep an eye on the ball and see how the defenders are rushing out. We practised it endlessly, so that we really didn't need the ear-pieces any more.

Most innovations arise to solve a problem. So a crisis is the perfect time for innovation. And I have learned that the best sources of new material may not be in your own sector or your own sport. The best innovations can be found elsewhere. The ice jackets used by the soldiers in Iraq and by Anky van Grunsven's horses. Robert Eenhoorn's signals. The ear-pieces from the Tour de France. Lots of innovations don't come from the coach anyway, but from the players – your 'staff'. They often have the best ideas.

A prime example of an innovation that the players insisted on was a penalty corner variant in which the ball was passed on twice, to the striker Kim Lammers. She would then hit the artificial grass really hard, splashing a load of water up in the defender's face and blinding her for a moment. Kim Lammers would incidentally miss the ball deliberately as part of the move. Finally Janneke Schopman would be at the far post to put the ball in. The players had experimented with the move at their club.

I didn't think much of the idea. It was never going to work. "Too complicated, too many actions that can go wrong. But go on," I said. "Show us."
And it worked. During the World Cup in 2006, we played England, who had the world's best penalty corner defence. Thanks to the kamikaze defender who rushed out to block the shot, we had trouble scoring against them. So we used the splash variant: goal by Janneke Schopman, 1-0. And it was the only goal of the game. Even the sports programme on TV fell for it, with the commentator that evening saying, "A horrible mistake by Kim Lammers, a complete air shot, but luckily it goes to Janneke Schopman who scores!"
But we knew better. After the match, the coaches from a couple of other countries came to me to compliment me on it. "The best corner I've ever seen," said one. "Marc, you're a genius."
I said that the players deserved the credit for that one, because they'd thought it up themselves. "Marc, you're too modest," said my colleagues. "Players don't come up with things like that." I thought, "That's nice – it just shows that their development is still some way behind ours..."

Being a hockey player didn't mean I couldn't find innovation in my own sport. My way of running in at a penalty corner to distract the opposition keeper worked very well and became famous (before being banned!) as 'lammeren'. My revolutionary hockey stick, later to become famous (before being banned!) as the 'Sinterklaasstick' for its bishop's crosier shape, was more than just a marketing stunt. So you can see that people on the workshop floor often come up with very specific innovations, but that genuinely new ways of thinking have to come from elsewhere. Thinking outside the box.

How can you tell whether an innovation is going to be a success if you've never done it before? When you start something, you also know that it might go pear-shaped. But if you try ten things and five of them work, then that's still a great deal better than nothing.

There are sectors in the business world that are in trouble now and that should really be looking at sectors where things are going nicely. Respond to what happens around you. It's all doom and gloom among the estate agents because house sales have dropped so dramatically. But there's another trend showing that people are going out less and cooking at home more. The estate agent in my town has closed half the office and started up a shop selling all sorts of items relating to eating and cooking. "Enjoy!" And it's doing very well. That's the kind of thing I mean.
If I were selling cars right now, I'd say it's time to clear out half my showroom and start selling bicycles. It's a crisis, so bikes will soon be coming back in. Lots of sectors do well during a recession too. Have a good look at why – and make the most of it! You need guts too. If you wait too long, the resources needed for the switchover will be gone. So take action, rather than waiting for the crisis to blow over.

Above all, innovation costs energy. People are usually happiest doing the same today as they did the day before. But if you want to progress, you'll have to make efforts to improve on the day before. I started doing just that after Athens in 2004. But it seems I didn't do it properly, or not thoroughly enough. So I went and talked to people, visited coaches throughout the world, and started studying theories and methods. Myers-Briggs and action typing, circles of influence, core quadrants, neurolinguistic programming. Reading, questioning, discussing. Looking to see where another two per cent might be obtained. I heard that PSV trained wearing vests with a GPS system built in. So I hopped into the car and went to the Herdgang training complex in Eindhoven. Then we started using the GPS system for the Dutch hockey team too and it showed us that we had to change our sprint training. We practised thirty-metre sprints, but the analysis of the GPS data showed that a sprint in a match was never more than fourteen metres. So we started training for fifteen-metre sprints and we did get quicker at those. All that innovation costs energy, particularly because you don't know beforehand what will work and what won't.

You therefore also end up pumping a lot of time and energy into things that will ultimately prove no use. If you aren't ready to do that, you will not find those two per cent gains either. People often think that innovation is going to cost them money. But that's the last thing you should be thinking about. The best innovations are not about money at all. They are about recognising an opportunity in a crisis. The money follows the ideas, not the other way round. When I went to Phonac for the ear-pieces that got us the second spot at the 2002 World Cup, I promised then that I would name them as the makers once it became public knowledge that we were using the earpieces. Phonac invested two years in the development. It didn't cost the hockey association a penny. This is something else you see more often in times of crisis: the barter economy – business swaps and favours. I scratch your back, you scratch mine. Cooperation becomes more important again.

Being convincing, webcams and open curtains

Innovating also means convincing people. Every time I came up with something new, I had to convince the board of directors of the hockey association. And I had to convince my coaching staff and the players too, of course. But you have to know how to break it to them. In my opinion, companies often force innovations upon employees, those innovations are implemented too soon, and they are presented poorly. People are sometimes only informed by e-mail that a new working method or system will be introduced. And could they switch to using the new systems from next week onwards. Good luck! You can compare it to buying a new CD player. You don't take the time to read the manual in detail to make sure you know how everything works.

No, just start using it right away! A year later you still don't know how the equipment works. Take your time for it.
If I had simply handed out eight earphones to my team at that time, everyone would have said, "Nonsense, we're not going to do that." With Mijntje Donners at the front of the queue. But because I presented my suggestion step by step, she became the ambassador for the idea!

A garage owner in the north of the country had concluded from a customer satisfaction survey that many customers thought that their garage bills were rather high. It was sometimes hard for them to realise what had to be done to the car and they were left with the feeling that they were being taken for a ride. That entrepreneur then decided to hang up webcams in his workshop. From then on he told his customers when their car was on the lift and customers could use a login code and watch their car was repaired on the Internet.
I think it's a nice example of handling a crisis in a clever way. Customers not trusting you any more are a problem that you should not underestimate. The media jumped all over it and the story was in all the papers. It wasn't the webcams themselves but the publicity that caused an enormous increase in new custom. His idea turned out to be so successful that a point came when he wasn't able to handle the work any longer. Although I wouldn't be surprised if only a few customers actually watched their cars on the webcams at all. Yet thanks to those webcams, the customers trusted the garage owner and that solved his problem of the allegedly high bills. An additional benefit was that his mechanics were aware of the webcams too and started to behave better, did not spend too long drinking coffee, left their earrings at home and worked more carefully.

When we won gold in Beijing, I knew that I had accomplished my four-year mission. But it isn't until now, in 2009, that I can finally point out where and why things worked out. You lack the overview if you're in the middle of the process. You are focused on doing the right things, but will it all work out?

Only when the crisis is over will you be able to see what you did well to survive the crisis. At this moment, more than a year after the Games, I'm particularly trying to determine the things that I knew beforehand would work out well. That may allow me to overcome the next crisis. Or I can help others to combat their crises.
Creativity in finding solutions is very important. But I want to prevent managers and directors from having the opportunity to play down the problems by saying, "But I'm not creative!"

My own creativity is based on two things: curiosity and recognising the right question. Strip a problem down to the bones: only then will you see the question that you actually want to answer. "We have to increase our turnover" is not the actual problem. "How can we turn the customers' mistrust into something that will give us *more* work?" like that garage owner and his webcams. Those are the real questions. So, the secret of combating a crisis often isn't in the creativity of the solution, but in the quality of the question. Ask the right questions. Curiosity will help you overcome a crisis.

The first two matches in Beijing were played in the morning at half past eight. Meals and preparations included, that meant that the players had to get up at five. We were due to play the third match in the evening. The swimmers had told us that that they had made detailed studies of how to wake up. A lot of the swimming events were also held early in the morning. The best way to wake up is with natural light. Maarten van der Weijden, who later became the Olympic 10km swimming champion, used an alarm clock with a light and even glasses with lights. Light activates the human energy management mechanisms. So we decided to sleep with the curtains open for the first two matches, as the sun in China was rising as early as five at that time. You'll wake up naturally. We had already tried it during the first few days of our stay in China. So when I asked the players to leave the curtains open on the evenings before the matches in question, nobody thought that it was weird. And I gained another two per cent.

It wasn't only open curtains only that broadened our view. We improved our video analyses too, time after time.
We had used video analysis regularly for years. Recordings are analysed by specialists and shown to the team during the preparations for a subsequent match.

However, for the Olympics we also used real-time video analyses. During the match, images from strategically placed cameras were sent to a laptop that displayed the images with a delay of ten seconds. That let us to watch replays of match situations immediately during the match. And we could also categorise those images too – opportunities, marking errors, and so forth. It meant we could show fragments of things they had done well or wrongly to players who were sitting on the bench for a while when players were substituted. We had a problem in midfield during the final of the World Cup in Madrid. Our midfield began marking every time the central midfield of Australia moved. It created openings that were used by Australia to pass the ball to their attackers. We fell for this trick time after time. I used the real-time video analysis to show my centre midfielder what was happening. After that, she filled the gap because she knew that the ball would not be passed to her direct opponent on the far left of the midfield. Problem solved.
Not many people know about this video system. Our opponents must have wondered sometimes what that box, that laptop and that antenna were for. Well, it was for immediate analysis, during the match itself.
These alternatives can also be used in the business world. Imagine you're having a conversation with a client. He asks about the status of a product. Shouldn't it be possible to contact the production department using your laptop or PDA, so that you can close a sales deal on the spot? The technology exists. We only need the will to use it. I'm not a technical expert, I'm just asking the question: "This is what I want to know. I think you can make this, can't you?" And then the technical experts start working on it. Right now, video analysis experts from the world of hockey are at the football club AZ Alkmaar. They were called in by the

manager, Louis van Gaal. And we've seen what AZ did the next season: national champions in 2009. Louis has now taken his hockey video-analyst with him to Bayern Munich.

Video, copying and failure

We used video analysis in a variety of ways. For our own play, both tactically and technically. For studying our opponents. And also for individual team members. My players all received a digital dossier that they could access over the Internet, with pictures of their direct opponent for the next match. "These are 25 moves by Aymar, the central midfielder of Argentina. Have a good look at how she takes the ball, where she takes the ball, what she can't handle, what her strengths are."

And then I asked my players, "What do you think is the best way of stopping her?"

We went to extraordinary lengths in our video analysis. We even analysed the referees. How they reacted, how they interpreted events. You may think that it's almost impossible to exert influence on referees, but that's not true. If you know how they react, you, as a player on the pitch, can respond to that. You detect patterns. There was one referee who very often let play continue after fouls. You can object or continue playing, keeping your concentration. We scored a goal because of that. At the Olympics we had two referees in our first match who we knew were non-nonsense and strict. If you let this annoy you, things will go wrong. In this case we knew exactly what was going to happen. And the team had already prepared themselves for it before the match. Did we go any further? Yes. We also talked to the judges, who were in the stands to judge the referees. We asked them what they would be paying particular attention to. In Beijing, we knew that the referees had instructions to interrupt the match as little as possible for small fouls that did not create any advantage. If you know things like that, you can use them to benefit your team. I wouldn't be surprised if the players only realise we did that when they read this. Take note: a good lawyer analyses the judge. A good entrepreneur analyses the rules. And makes use of them.

I also used video as a way of manipulating people. When I was with the Dutch team I once worked them extremely hard for two days before to a practice match against England, a team that was physically very strong. I was almost certain that we would lose this match after exerting ourselves so much. And we did. After the match, I showed the team an overview of all things that went wrong. "Look, this is where you're too to the ball; that's where you left a gap. See? There was no link with mid-field..."
It was a preconceived plan to get everyone focused once more. Everyone had both feet on the ground again.

Video analysis is both a source of information and a source of inspiration. I often used images for training specific techniques. If I saw Shabbas (a top Pakistani hockey player) use a lift technique, a way of flicking the ball up and passing the opponent, I would showed it to the players: "This is what we are going to practise today." Recognition is so important. If I want to teach you something, you have to know why first. It's easy to prove that using video. I can let you see what the purpose is. I reckon that I know what is wrong when something isn't going well in eighty per cent of the cases. But I want the camera to confirm it. It never lies. And I can only see that other twenty per cent after a few replays. In one match we saw that attackers were managing to get into the circle easily down the right, but that it kept coming to nothing. There were considerably fewer attacks down the left, but they were much more effective. In the first instance you might expect to create opportunities when attacking down the right. But video analysis may show that it's better to opt for fewer attacks down the left as long as they're more effective. You can't see that with your own eyes immediately, because you are in the middle of a match. Video analysis makes you take a step back. Eventually a lot of our video analyses were given to the hockey association for youth hockey training. So we're making the best possible use of that instrument, even for training the next generation of internationals.

Why not make a video analysis of your sales staff? Or of your production leader during a meeting with his staff? You'll see more. On top of that, it can help you to make sales staff aware of things that they might be doing unintentionally. Video analysis helps you optimise the efficiency of your people.
Or why invite hundreds of clients to a reception if you can organise a series of seminars with ten groups of ten people, where the quality and effectiveness can be much higher? Make an analysis of the effectiveness of your efforts and you will make the proper choices. And what about video in business? I think that in ten years' time, negotiation talks will be recorded. Both parties will be going home with a copy of the same visual material. You can analyse what went well or wrong at home.

What if your competitor copies the idea? Don't worry. Continue your approach until it's no longer efficient. Australia had cooling jackets too at the Olympics in China. It's okay – why shouldn't they? It didn't make me decide to stop using those jackets. We kept our efficiency. If everyone had used those cooling jackets, we might have had to come up with something new again.
It's the biggest compliment you can get. If your competitors are copying you, it means that they think your approach is better than theirs. But make sure that you overcome the initial problems of such a new approach before they do. By the way, copying everything a competitor does is difficult, even in business.

And what if an idea is not successful? You'll gain authority by having adopted an emotionally vulnerable position. If things work out wrong, just admit it. I apologised on several occasions, every time things went wrong. You'll earn respect. If you show understanding and compassion, you will win people's sympathy. I often see managers doing the opposite. They think that adopting a vulnerable position undermines your authority. So they shout as loud as they can to make clear how they want things to be and they don't want to hear any objections. You're not allowed to show weakness.

I took a training session in freezing cold weather once and two players fell ill. "You should have dressed warmer," is what that kind of manager would have said. I apologised and admitted that it wasn't very clever of me to decide to train under the circumstances. If you are a manager who only shows his strong side, you'll end up with problems. Confirming the emotions of your staff will help you further. But focus on the commitment you want to get from your people.

From an eight to a ten and the thick hockey-regulations book

I've never won a match based on the weak elements in my team. Changing an eight out of ten into full marks does more than changing a four into a six. That's just a way of making sure you end up being average at everything. You can only excel by being outstanding at something. Sometimes our team would discuss a single action in a match for more than half an hour. We would watch it on video and analyse the situation extensively: "What could be done better next time?" or "What exactly was it that went so well?" There is not much time for evaluation in the business world. They say that it is inefficient. On the contrary, in the long run it's much more important than keeping on doing what you've always done. So look in particular at things that are going well!

If you deliberately train the aspects people are not skilled at, you will unconsciously start using skills that people are not competent at. So if you know that you're not good at something, you will unconsciously become worse at it. You should therefore work above all on what you're unconsciously competent at, and you'll unconsciously end up doing what you're good at. Sylvia Karres was our centre forward. Her ball control on the backhand was poor. We thought we had to practise that. And time after time, the ball was miscontrolled. Other team members doubted whether she was good enough for the Dutch team. "If you're not even able to control the ball on your backhand properly..."

We did exercises in which all team members had to pass backhands to her. We were intentionally working on what she was not skilled at. And you can guess what happened during the match. Everybody was passing to her backhand again. Standing on the sidelines, I kept on shouting: "Not the backhand! Not the backhand!" At that time, I hadn't had any neurolinguistic programming (NLP) lessons, otherwise I would have known that our brains can't handle the word 'not' so well. If I tell you not to think of a pink elephant, it's plain impossible.

It was a long time before I understood how to deal with Sylvia. I thought: practice, practice, practice. But it didn't really work. I wanted to get my team members' four-out-of-ten scores up to sixes. Sylva eventually made me change my mind. Such a talented centre forward, but only scoring one or two goals in a tournament – how was that possible? She totally lost her self-confidence.

Then we started to re-evaluate. I asked Sylvia, "How would you like the ball played to you?" She said she preferred taking a really hard ball aimed at her right foot, so that she could score a tap-in on her forehand, directly from the pass. What happened? At the World Cup in Madrid she scored seven goals, five of them tap-ins like that. We had played to her competences and everyone was aware of that. Sylvia was top scorer at the tournament.

What had happened here? I had reversed the sequence of talent development! Usually, a didactic process includes the following steps:
Step 1: you're unconsciously incompetent: four out of ten.
Step 2: you become consciously incompetent: six out of ten.
Step 3: you become consciously competent: eight out of ten.
Step 4: you become unconsciously competent: ten out of ten.

From that moment on, I always started with step 3: the things that you already score eight out of ten for. I turned those into a ten: step 4.

With a ten, if you're good at something, you accumulate self-confidence. Enough self-confidence that you'll spontaneously come up with idea to change the fours (step 1) into sixes (step 2). Maartje Goderie was our fastest player in the midfield. Her tens were controlling the ball on the run and then using her speed to get past the opponent, and getting balls simply due to her pace and speed of reaction. Her fours? The backhand. A few weeks before the Olympics in Beijing she came to me. "Marc, should I do some work on my backhand shot?"
I consulted Rico Schuijers, the mental coach: "Marc, that's great. If the girls have the self-confidence to come up personally with the idea of working on their weaknesses, you should be very glad about that!"
In the final against China, Maartje Goderie scored the 2-0 ten minutes before the end of the match. Take a look at those pictures again; look at her face just after she's scored. The astonishment in her eyes: "Hey – I scored with a backhand!"

In business, you often see that people start tinkering with everything that isn't going well. Everything that is going well is ignored and left alone. If you want to make improvements, you'll be more efficient if you work on the things that you're competent at. You'll gain more confidence, more commitment, more pleasure. You can't work on the things that are not going well until then. People don't dare show their vulnerable side until they feel confident and certain about themselves. Change some eights out of ten into full marks first; you can only try to boost a four into a six after that.

My left back in Beijing, Maartje Paumen, was a rather slow defender who could take a devastating short corner. Of course, I could have worked endlessly on Maartje's sprints. I'm sure she would have become a little bit faster, but you can never turn a tortoise into a hare. She was never going to be fast enough to deal with our opponents' fastest centre forwards.

I still played her, though. After all, she had an excellent penalty corner and had been taking them since she was twelve, which gave her a lead over everyone. She was simply the best at that. We focused entirely on those corners with her. Day after day, we trained with Toon Siepman. With help from TNO, the Dutch Institute for Applied Scientific Research, we were able to use the latest technology and work out that corner to perfection. Computer animations, mathematical calculations, knee-angle calculations, spinal torsion, drag forces – it was one big laboratory.

Outsiders thought this was weird. “Okay, so you’ll have someone who takes the corners. But at left back, any opponent can run straight through your defence”. We solved that problem in a different way. In the centre of the defence was Minke Booij, who has pace. I shifted her somewhat more to the left, making sure that Maartje Paumen had cover at all times. At that time Minke was the best defender in the world. On the right side I had two very quick defenders, Eva de Goede or Sophie Polkamp, who could easily use their speed to fill any gaps there. And the results were there for all to see. Maartje Paumen became the all-time top scorer at an Olympic tournament with eleven goals.

The innovation and improvement also applied to the coaching staff for Beijing. The coaching staff for the 2004 Olympics in Athens had a different setup than the team that I took with me to China. It not only had different people, but a different profile of characters and ages. In 2004, I had a team of perfect hockey coaches. They were all energetic but relatively young and inexperienced, and so they also kept meddling with each other’s tasks. There were moments that some of those coaches seemed to want to be the manager; every now and then, they even shared their views with team members. Not much empathy, no arms round the shoulders or things like that. Our commitment as the coaching staff was so intense that there were times that we did not see the boundaries of our own roles any more.

As a team’s coach, you have to support your team through the disappointments. This coaching team overreacted when the disappointments came. After the final in Athens, the coaching staff

were angry and frustrated when the team lost. They should have been supporting the players instead.
The various people on the coaching staff nearly all had much the same knowledge. I had chosen the team myself. I made mistakes in doing so. The association had allowed me to make my own choices. I myself was the problem here; the staff were all capable people. But they did not make a good team for that hockey squad. I sometimes still blame myself for that. When we were on our way to the Olympics in 2008, the members of my coaching staff complemented each other much better. One knew what the other didn't, and vice versa. In 2004, I had wanted to quit my job as a national team manager; it was hard for me to overcome the disappointment. I extended my contract to four years, at the insistence of my team and the association. But the players also immediately added, "We would like to keep working with Marc, but only with another backup team."
André Bolhuis, president of the hockey association, then helped me set up my new team. "Why don't you just put together my coaching staff?" I asked him. My team then started including older people; I reckon the average age must have increased by 25 years. People I didn't know at all. More empathy, more experience, more atmosphere, more variation. Bolhuis even came up with Rob Bianchi, the hockey coach who had called me a fool in the press! It became clear to me that I was much better off with this diversity. And that the team of coaches had become a challenge for me as well now. They disagreed with me more often. These people also took their responsibility; they spoke clearly and did not doubt.

How far will you go in a crisis situation? Which innovations will be implemented and which won't? Where are your ethical boundaries? Companies are also wrestling with the same thing now. You could see it in the banking community – and what happened? A lot more regulations, more legislation, more defined procedures. When I look at the book of rules for the game of hockey ten years ago, it's just a thin booklet. Today it's a thick tome.

There are people who, when asked who made that book of rules so thick, answer decisively: "Marc Lammers..."

Opportunity 5: Keep on innovating and don't just look in your own back yard

Innovation costs energy, not money. Money comes from good ideas, not the other way round. During the eight years that I was the manager of the Dutch women's hockey team, I didn't get my best ideas from the world of hockey. On the contrary, I got my best ideas from outside the hockey community. From other sports. If you're trying to find a solution for your crisis, don't go looking for it in your own back yard. Try to find it elsewhere. I used innovations from horse racing, cycling, baseball, football, swimming and other sources. Outside the box.

4

THE MORE YOU MEASURE, THE MORE YOU KNOW

We knew a lot about our players. Everything had been mapped out. Oxygen uptake, temperature, pulse rate, fluid content, weight, muscle mass, iron level, acidification, agility, sprinting speed – in fact, everything you need to know to give players the best medical guidance. It turned out, for instance, that we had to submit a request four months before the Games for any team members who used inhalers. We submitted requests for three of our players, because investigations and our previous visits to China had shown that they were slightly asthmatic. We also knew that having a low fat percentage would be very important in the heat of Beijing. But measurements earlier years had already taught us that girls gain weight when they start living on their own. Prior to the Olympics, we asked a number of parents to keep their daughter at home for another year. Precisely because of the better nutrition, for instance. But you can only do things like that if you have a database of statistics covering many years. For me, the 'physical' dimension really comes first when you have to set priorities on the preparations for a tournament as tough as the Olympics. The 'mental' part comes second on my list, followed by 'tactical' and finally 'technical'. After all, if you can't play hockey, you won't be part of the team in the first place. The physical and mental strength eventually brought us victory.

Statistical parameters won't be reliable until you have made at least eight measurements. You won't see any trends or developments until then. I always think that the business and commerce sectors hardly use any measurements. And if they do, it's just a couple of times, then a few changes are made and that's that.

Companies really know very little about their competitors. We produced internal and external 'benchmarks' for our team members. The internal part was a comparison against their own performances and previous statistics. The external part was a comparison against our opponents.

We made a relatively large effort to optimise the performance levels of our team members statistically. During the preparations, the team doctor asked the players, "When do you feel best? When are you at your strongest?"
It turned out that some of the players said that they felt at their strongest when they were menstruating. We even included this in the preparations for matches. But exactly the opposite applied to other members of our team. It was just a matter of keeping using the pill. All those details resulted in the best possible team performance. I keep saying, "Fifty times two per cent improvement is one hundred per cent better too!"

They also often say you're a pain in the neck, a bit of a bastard, if you drag people along in your own perfectionism. Gaining that two per cent over and over again is a continuous process. I also got the players to watch video images on the Internet that we had selected for that specific team member. Later on, we could tell if she had done it or not. We talked to team members about it. I'm sure they must have thought that it all went too far sometimes, and that they were entitled to a little bit of leisure time as well. But I never stopped gaining that two per cent time and time again. I was often able to do so, but sometimes not. Each two per cent, each successful small change eventually accumulates to give an overall approach. Ice baths, exercises, personal development plans: players who did not accept this method had to leave the team.

Opportunity 6: Fifty times two per cent is a hundred per cent too

As a manager or supervisor, why not make a list of fifty things that could each improve the process by two per cent? Make sure they're measurable and tick them off, and present them to your staff. Show them how you are dealing with the crisis.

In fact, I would have liked to know much more and keep even more statistics. But I 'only' saw that team nine times a week during the training sessions. You might say that that's a lot, but it isn't really. Not for all the things we had to do. So I had to set priorities for the statistics we collected. I would have loved to have been able to use the 'Omega-wave', a measuring device used for astronauts. A little box around the wrist measures the peaks in your pulse rate. It helps you to determine how far you can go in someone's training. AC Milan use it too. You can determine the ideal training intensity for that specific player, based on that measurement. But unfortunately, it turned out to be very complicated after all.

Take the Dutch Olympic football team in Beijing. You could actually see that those players weren't properly fit. I'm not trying to snipe at my fellow national team manager Foppe de Haan. But we focused on physical fitness for the women's hockey team, to an almost extreme degree. Both Foppe's players and ours trained in the NOC*NSF climate chambers at Papendal. I can still see the footballer Gerald Sibon coming out of that room: "Oh, it's not all that hard..." But you're only in that stifling and humid atmosphere for two hours; in China you're in it 24 hours a day. Prior to the tournament, the Olympic football team had never been to China. To me this seems unbelievable, despite the undoubtedly busy competition schedules of the footballers. Companies that take up the fight against competitors when they're not in shape during a crisis won't stand a chance.

Bribery, emotion and blind penalties

We wanted to exclude every possible uncertainty. We even bribed guards for that. We were in Beijing in 2007 and there we were, standing at the gate of the Olympic Village, which was under construction. We wanted to have a look inside, but that was not allowed, of course.

So we gave one of the guards fifty euros and were allowed to look around. We took pictures, produced thorough descriptions of the setup and had a look inside the apartments. We knew what we needed to take and what we didn't.

As we had already been to China twice in the years prior to the Olympics, we also knew all about the traffic there. How long it takes to get anywhere. What you have to do if the bus doesn't turn up or if it's late. If the team members haven't experienced it before, the stress of it all could affect them. But we knew just how it worked. During a training camp in 2007, I played a joke by getting the bus that was to pick us up for the session to arrive half an hour later. You could see the team members enjoying the sun during that half an hour... and the training session was a complete flop. So what did they do from then on? They wore caps, took their umbrellas with them, stayed in the shade and made sure they drank enough. "We're not here for the sunbathing!"

China was nothing but heat and smog. There wouldn't be any rain there. During the preparations in the Netherlands, we played a friendly against the USA. It was held at the HDM ground in The Hague. In pouring rain. The players asked if the match could be cancelled. I said, "No, we're going to play! This could happen in China too!" The media jumped on that one. Marc Lammers had gone mad. He was preparing for the Olympics in China in the pouring rain. Weather forecasters in China were interviewed and they confirmed that there wouldn't be any rain in China during the Olympic Games. Well, we all know what happened: it was bucketing down during the first match against South Africa. My players did not make a single complaint, not even at breakfast. Nobody was bothered about the bad weather. Later on, the racing cyclists were heard complaining about the rainfall. They had not taken it into account. But we had. The crisis had turned into an opportunity. After all, the big advantage of a crisis is that your competitor is dealing with the same thing.

Finding the right balance between emotion and rational analysis is very difficult. When are statistics crucial? When are emotions crucial? One of my assistants had studied the statistics. He had worked out everything, knew all the details. Right up to how the opponents took penalties. But if you really want to use those statistics, you have to consider the emotions as well. Some players take penalties differently when there is a lot of pressure, compared to a situation where scoring is not so important. If you manage to include those emotional aspects in your statistics, the instrument will be absolutely invaluable.

I have found out that my coaching method has benefited a lot from the capability of switching between emotions and logic. I take a lot of decisions based on emotions. But I do always like to substantiate them using statistics. Sometimes I will go for a cold and statistical approach, but in other cases I will respond to the emotions within the team. There is no clear-cut rule, but you will get the best results if you manage to switch effectively between the two worlds of analysis and gut feelings. Guus Hiddink is another: he can be a professor, but he can also be a friend. He showed that at Chelsea too.

Changes in the coaching can cause confusion. But on the other hand, confusion causes agitation and agitation helps keep people sharp. I used the two styles, logic and emotion, in that way too. I have been deliberately unreasonable at times, for instance by insisting on an extremely heavy training session. Cursing and swearing. They though I'd gone mad. I also wrote personal notes to all the players when we were in Beijing. Switching between statistics and emotions makes sure that everyone stays focused.
If your leadership is based on logic only, you're short-changing not only yourself but those who work for you too. But if your leadership is based on emotions alone, you'll be looking for a new job very soon... The gains to be made from a crisis come from the way that you coach, from your management of the software – the people. Nothing to do with the hardware.

Training in Rotterdam, 2007. "As part of the preparations for Beijing, I went back to doing the training sessions myself more." Photo: Ben Haeck

Press conference before the European Championships in Manchester. From left to right: Marilyn Agliotti, Marc Lammers, Minke Booij, Fatima Moreira de Melo and Minke Smabers. Photo: Ben Haeck

The 2007 European Championships in Manchester. National team manager Marc Lammers, his assistant Max Caldas and Bart Looije look pensive. The Netherlands have just lost the final against Germany. Photo: Ben Haeck

"I took a training session in freezing cold weather once and two players fell ill. I apologised and admitted that it wasn't very clever of me to decide to train under the circumstances." From left to right: Marc Lammers and Maartje Paumen. Photo: Ben Haeck

Back to basics in Oman. Sitting in the sand, along with the locals.

Sports psychologist Rico Schuijers went to Oman too and spoke with all the players individually. "Marc, you'll only see things clearly again in two weeks' time."

There we were, all of us, staring into that fire. The Olympic flame – "The Road to F(l)ame"?

Oman was a decisive point during the preparations for the Olympics in China. "I was very insecure, not convinced it would work out right." From left to right: Janneke Schopman, Maartje Paumen, Marc Lammers and Max Caldas.

We spent that evening as a group, watching the opening ceremony on the TV in our very own 'Holland House'. Then they all went to bed, to read those notes…

We were visited by the Dutch prime minister, Jan-Peter Balkenende, during one of our training sessions in Beijing.

The temperatures and timings for our system of ice baths were actually fine-tuned individually to the players. But we simply told the Argentineans that we went and sat in iced water for twenty minutes.

Every day we had to take a luggage trolley loaded with kit to the training sessions. Luckily, our special cooling machine was allowed to stay in the hockey stadium. Innovation can be hard work.

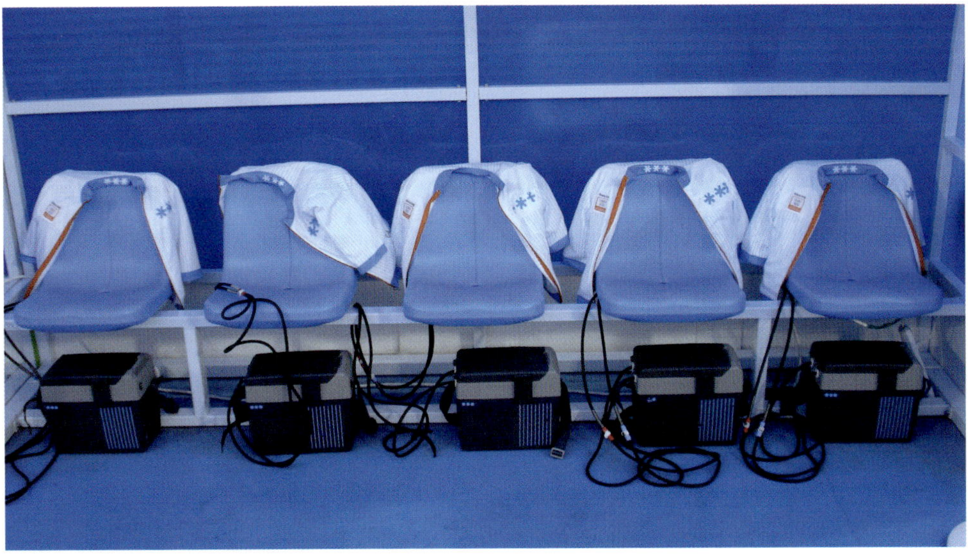

I got the idea for the ice jackets from some Dutch soldiers who had been to Iraq. Anky van Grunsven, triple gold medallist in the dressage, was also using cooling jackets for the horses. The jackets were connected up to a cooling element on a belt.

Even the team manager has to cool off occasionally. Here I am wearing a cooling jacket at a training session.

ROAD O

The Road to F(l)ame. Source: Verdieping 10

(L)AME

TOELICHTING

Het team is meer dan een optelsom van individuen. Samen is niet alleen, Eén voor allen: allen voor één en hart voor het team.
Proces: Up's en down's.
The Greatest Glorie is not never falling, but rising up every time you fall.
Wij gaan voor het einddoel, in voor- en tegenspoed, in goede en slechte tijden, tot en met de sluiting......
Wat is hierop jullie antwoord?

We trained day in, day out in China. Even on the rest days. 'Tapering on', working up to the final.

We only had one keeper in China: Lisanne de Roever (left). We didn't have a spare goalie on the bench. Our second keeper, Floortje Engels (right) was in China, but stayed outside the Olympic village.

Marc Lammers is apparently still calm after reaching the Olympic final in China. His players have just beaten Argentina 5-2. From left to right: Sophie Polkamp, Maartje Goderie, Marc Lammers and Eefke Mulder. Photo: Ben Haeck

"I know successful coaches who act like one of the team. But that's not my way of doing things, though I did do it every now and again..." Marc Lammers is listening to Maartje Paumen, Lisanne de Roever, Wieke Dijkstra and Eefke Mulder at a training session at the 2006 World Championships in Madrid. Photo: Ben Haeck

Marc Lammers after the Netherlands-Australia game. Confidence is growing: "We were in a flow." Photo: Ben Haeck

The Beijing Olympics in 2008. Some of the Dutch team's staff are watching tensely as the national anthems are played for the Netherlands and Korea. From left to right: Irene Engelbertink, Sandra Le Poole, Peter Verzijden and Marc Lammers. Photo: Ben Haeck

"I was more cheering them on. They took their own decisions. That gave me real satisfaction..." Marc Lammers during the Olympic final, Netherlands versus China. Photo: Ben Haeck

Maartje Paumen was the top scorer at the Olympic tournament. "Full marks instead of eight out of ten…" Photo: Ben Haeck

The girls also came up with a fourth team value: "We want to be fit and we want to look good." Photo: Ben Haeck

The 2008 Olympic Champions! From left to right: Johannes Veen, Sandra Le Poole, Max Caldas, Maartje Paumen, Minke Smabers, Lars Gillhaus, Lisanne de Roever, Janneke Schopman, Maartje Goderie, Floortje Engels, Bart Looije, Naomi van As, Miek van Geenhuizen, Eva de Goede, Ellen Hoog, Minke Booij, Liedewij Welten, Irene Engelbertink, Sophie Polkamp, Wieke Dijkstra, Fatima Moreira de Melo, Marilyn Agliotti, Eefke Mulder, Kelly Jonker, Peter Verzijden and Marc Lammers. Photo: Ben Haeck

A crisis is the perfect time for innovation. Even before the Olympics in Athens, I had been using video goggles to watch repeats of our opponents' defence when we were taking short corners. Photo: Jeroen van Bergen

Marc Lammers is currently making efforts to help young people in the Netherlands. He developed the Marc Lammers Plaza specially for children: integrating outdoor play and games computers. This is a modern and exciting way of encouraging children to get more exercise. A Marc Lammers Plaza consists of four separate play elements. The first Marc Lammers Plaza has already arrived – and may there be many more of them! More information is available on www.marclammers.nl/marc-lammers-plaza.

There will always still be a missing link, even after you've got statistics on everything: the emotions. How could I control, measure and influence human emotions? Peter Murphy, the former manager of the national women's volleyball team, introduced me to his method of 'Total Coaching'. The players' characters play a key role in this method. Total Coaching is based on the theory and personality typologies of Myers-Briggs, known as Action Typing. Action typing gives you insights into your own nature as well as other people's. It created acceptance within our group. They now knew each other's good and bad sides. Then you no longer have to get annoyed by the bad sides of other players or colleagues. On one occasion the players had to sit across the table facing each other. Each time they changed seats, the question they both had to keep answering was: "State five characteristics of the player facing you: one negative characteristic and four positive characteristics about technique, tactics, and physical and mental aspects." That meant that all players not only knew what others considered to be points they could improve on, but also in particular what aspects the players thought other team members were good at.
Recognise, acknowledge, accept. You can't make use of the things a person excels at until then.
But what do you see happening all too often? We list other people's weak points, tell them where improvements could be made, criticise them. It's not very inspiring and it also undermines our confidence in each other. Too often, we judge people by what they say, how they look and how they act, without knowing what triggered that judgement. The four Myers-Biggs types gave the players the 'tools' to be able to talk to each other about irritations and appreciation. The time that we spent on that has been as valuable as the training sessions on the pitch.

The Action Type theory classifies people's attitude to life and their behavioural style into four measuring points:

1. what do people focus their attention on? *Extrovert or introvert?*
2. how do people process information? *Observation or intuition?*

3. how do people take decisions? *Reflection or emotion?*
4. how do people respond to the outside world? *Control or perception?*

During the initial years that I was the Dutch team manager, I always had the idea that working with women was like skating on very thin ice. As long as you keep moving fast enough, things will work out all right. But if you stand still, you'll fall though the ice. Delving into concepts such as action typing taught me that it's better to make sure the ice is thick enough. That makes it possible for you to stop and think about important matters, such as behaviour and character. Knowing your players' characters helps you with your coaching, helps you build your team.
The team members first started to recognise things in each other, and then progressed to acknowledging and accepting these aspects. Team members don't have to be best friends to play hockey together well. I had Miek van Geenhuizen and Fatima Moreira de Melo, the two biggest opposites in our team, share a room at several tournaments. Because they knew each other's nature, it was no longer a problem at all. Diversity is part of the strength of a team.
If you let your employees gain insights into the qualities and allergies of others, they will be able to recognise and acknowledge them in each other. That lets you make the best possible use of the diversity within your organisation, without running the risk that everything is kept covered up until it blows up in your face at an awkward moment.

Peter Murphy has worked with our keeper since 2003. They have analysed the penalties taken by Australia and Argentina using the action typing method, for instance. During the Olympic semi-final against Argentina, our keeper knew that so-and-so is an introverted player who takes decisions based on emotion, so she'll just wait until I've chosen a corner. So I'll stand my ground as long as possible. And then the Argentinean player missed her penalty, because our keeper stayed where she was. We won the penalty shoot-out, whereas we had been thoroughly beaten in 2002! We haven't lost a penalty shoot-out since 2002.

Before that, people had claimed that you couldn't train for penalties. Rubbish. But any such training does need this type of preparation.

We even practised taking penalties blindfolded. And you know what? Some of our players actually scored more often with a blindfold than without. If you're blindfolded, you have to visualise your goal. Where's the ball? Where's the goal? You can focus entirely on your technique. If you're not blindfolded, you get distracted by all the other things that you see. This was an ideal method for players who like to decide beforehand which corner to shoot at. Others, who like to see what the goalie is doing so that they can respond to that, didn't use this practice method. But then their characters were different. We knew what our team members did and did not liked when taking penalties. Some of them want you to shout "Come on", but others need to be left alone. You will increase the effectiveness of your team members if you respond to their behavioural style. Action typing gives you those insights.

If you know what motivates your team members, you can make the most of it. Companies and organisations do not look at people's behavioural styles enough. People are often tackled about their behaviour in the wrong way, which is counter-productive. If you know your team members' mental preferences and pet hates, you will be able to boost their effectiveness enormously.
But don't do anything that people cannot relate to. After four years of sessions, Rico Schuijers finally introduced the first relaxation exercises to our team. During these relaxation exercises, the girls had to focus on their respiration, close their eyes and concentrate on their inner 'me'. Sounds a bit woolly? If we had started out doing that, the players would certainly have immediately started querying it. But now they came up with questions like, "The only thing I still have trouble with is controlling my stress before the match."

It is important within companies and organisations too: make sure that your people understand your approach. Because if it's too extreme, everyone will quit. Managers have to implement changes step by step as well. Otherwise it won't work. *'Inch by inch'*, adding that two per cent each time.

Your own strength, satellites and the pointlessness of strength training

During the preparations for the Olympics, I found all sorts of fun ways to make my team stronger than all their competitors. I only took a single keeper to China; a second goalie was available, but she was not on the bench during the matches. All the other countries all had fourteen outfield players, one goalie and one reserve goalie. But I had one more outfield player, i.e. an advantage of seven per cent compared with the competitors. All the outfield players benefited from it, being able to rest just a little bit longer than their opponents when I was substituting players. It worked out great. Right through to the final, you could just see that my players were much fitter, and this strategy was one of the contributory factors. We worked that one out by basing it on our own strengths.

We also knew our opponents' strengths. If you don't know what your opponent is doing, you can't know what you have to do to be better than them. I got my players to ask the foreign members of their club teams questions: "Ask those Argentinean girls at your club how often they train each week." And then I added, "But if they ask you the same thing, never tell them everything about what we really do." That was how we found out that Germany and Australia used 'mental training' too.

Through our own observations we knew how often China's team trained, what they were doing and how long they trained. Through a kind of Google Earth Live. So we used satellite images to follow their training sessions in secret. We kept track of those sessions for weeks. It was done for us by people who had access to such systems. We also observed Australia and Argentina, who were our main competitors.

We found out that China had apparently not trained for two weeks. Later on it turned out that they had moved to a hall...
We kept training at different locations during all those years. Den Bosch, Tilburg, Amsterdam, Helmond, you name it. We did that to make sure that every player from every part of the country had the same amount of travel time. It also meant we were in different environments all the time, which prevented us from getting into a rut or accustomed to just one type of grass or synthetic pitch. If China had some poor bloke spying on us using satellite images, we must have driven him mad...

> ***Opportunity 7: Measure what you want to know***
>
> *Almost anything can be measured. You should not accept a lack of information during a crisis. Do it in a scientifically responsible way. Or however suits. Even if you spy on your competitors using Google Earth, you may gain valuable information from that. Chuck out all the figures and statistics that you don't need to know. Otherwise, before you know it, you'll start using them in your plans. Like the weather forecasts for China.*

NOC*NSF is making the case for having fixed training centres. I don't like that idea; it makes you feel as if you're in a prison. Make sure the routine is broken, always with a different lunch, a different table arrangement, a different hotel room, a different dressing room, a different pitch. Those satellite images gave me another reason for emphasising once again that you should change locations regularly. After all, that Google Earth technology is getting more and more sophisticated...

Among all those extreme forms of preparation, one we could have adopted might have been making an exact copy of the pitch in Beijing. But we didn't do that. It was done in 2000 though, when we made a copy of the pitch in Sydney. But what happened after two months? The Dutch weather caused the quality of the pitch to be so different from the one in Australia that it totally cancelled out the advantage of using an identical pitch.

To compensate for this, we trained on every type of synthetic grass pitch we could find in Holland during the preparations. We didn't want to get used to any one type of surface. And we didn't want to get used to the best possible playing conditions either.

By the way: companies nowadays seem to make a habit of holding meetings in expensive hotels and beautiful 'conference centres'. Why not go camping with your managers? Use a propane gas ring and make the coffee yourself! Hold meetings sitting round a campfire.

And now back to training on all types of synthetic grass... We were so good all round that we were eventually able to adapt to the Chinese pitch very well. It makes me think of our first match in Beijing, against South Africa. It never rains in August in China – except that one time. The rain came down in sheets. That meant that the pitch was quite different from what would usually be expected in China, but that didn't bother us at all.

It's easy to keep a count of penalty corners. It's also possible to count the times you enter the circle. Tactics are quantifiable too. I wanted to be the best at match analysis. That's why I had two assistants, real analysis experts. And the video people, of course. Those analyses came up with the weirdest statistics. They knew how often our opponents were dangerous when attacking down the right or down the left. They knew which players on the other teams preferred which passes, how they controlled the ball, which way they looked first when they had the ball. We used it all. If you know that the player you are marking always looks left after controlling the ball, you have to make sure that you're on the right, so you can knock the ball clear. That sort of stuff. Statistics give you insights about your competitors, which you can use to deal with your opponent more effectively.

Throughout the preparations we used evaluation forms that stated all our objectives: technical, tactical, physical and mental. The team members assessed themselves and I assessed them too. We talked openly about it.
In organisations, assessment interviews and job performance interviews are often an obligatory element. "He doesn't communicate well" is a common complaint. Okay, but what is it that he doesn't communicate well? Or doesn't communicate about? Such assessments have to be made concrete if you want to do anything with them. It is seldom the case that employees are asked to assess themselves. However, the points where my evaluation differed most from the player's personal assessment were often the most interesting items to talk about. Incidentally, you might want to know that I made my assessments without knowing the player's input beforehand.
You can score an 8 for 'physical' and a 4 for 'lifestyle'. Mental issues such as self-confidence often provide a variable picture that you can work on together.

Everyone had a personal development plan, which also used this feedback as one of its inputs. The players themselves stated which aspects they would like to work on. We used that evaluation method for four years. It lets you see demonstrable development in the players. Progress makes you feel confident about the future. As a team's manager, you should not only be able to show that players can turn an eight out of ten into a perfect score, but also how they should go about it. Coaching means taking people forward from 'wanting' to 'doing'.

The first four-year period, before Athens 2004, I mostly looked at the best players. During the preparations for China 2008, I used a different approach. I based it on the following question: which seven team members will be making a difference because of their unique and specific qualities? Who will be the key players? Who will stand out? One: the team's captain, Minke Booij – a world-class defender and a top-class personality.

Two: Janneke Schopman, a tactical all-rounder. Three: Maartje Paumen, the corner specialist. Then came Fatima Moreira de Melo, the mental and social captain. If you combine those players with Minke Smabers, who has tremendous stamina in midfield, then those excellent qualities can be combined into a team. Miek van Geenhuizen brought in her unique technical skill; Maartje Goderie added her speed and capacity to stop opponents effectively. The rest of the squad was based on aspects that would complement those seven. It led me to the most creative attackers, ones who were just not able to put the ball away. Ellen Hoog, Liedewij Welten and Naomi van As were the girls who could win the penalty corners that were then smacked into the goal by Maartje Paumen. The unique added value of Marilyn Agliotti, Eva de Goede, Sophie Polkamp, Eefke Mulder and Wieke Dijkstra was that they were able to play in several positions. Goalie Lisanne de Roever was not just the stopper for the team; she also knew how to adapt to the leadership roles of Minke and Janneke. They all had their weaknesses too, but those were compensated for by other players. We weren't going to win because we weren't good enough at the things that we weren't able to do. We were going to win because we were better at the things that we were able to do well. Perhaps Argentina had the better and more complete players all round. But they were easy to handle because they failed to compensate for each others' weaknesses.

The worse things get, the more (or the sooner) people start doing the same things. But if you keep on passing the ball from one side to the other, all you will end up doing is passing harder and faster. No: do something else, because you won't improve if you keep on doing the same things. NOC*NSF thought that I should give thirty per cent more strength training during the preparations for the Olympics in China. Studies had shown that strength training was underrated in team sports. They asked me to start working with it. But I didn't really see what good it would do. Power training, or strength training, is usually totally different from a match situation. What's the use of lifting weights at the gym, when what you need in a match is three-dimensional movement involving sprinting, ball control and maybe giving the opponent a slight push?

I also knew that Australia and China were physically stronger than us, and would be so no matter how hard we worked out at the gym. So I could choose between power training and making sure that we would be quicker. That's why my training focused on action speed and sprints. We specialised in 'playing hockey and not playing the opponent': by the time she wanted to start pushing and pulling, we had already got rid of the ball. So I said 'no' to the NOC*NSF philosophy, while respecting their opinion. Fortunately they also appreciated my approach.

Using any statistical means and any measuring device, I had been telling my players for four years that now was when they had to work on the feeling that they wanted to have later, on the day before the final. What would you like to be able to do technically, how strong would you like to be mentally, how fit would you like to feel? In fact, it's a translation of the objectives that you dream of, broken down into separate steps. Use it as the basis for defining your performance targets. You work backwards, calculating what you need to do now to reach that desired objective one day before the final. You start converting those performance targets for each segment into quantifiable exercises and training routines.

Although innovations are often permissible within companies, they do have to be viable right from the start. As a manager, you should have the nerve to invest in a poorer return at the start of an innovation. That lets you protect your staff against the preset result targets. If a new sales method is contrasted against the existing targets from the very first moment, that innovation will be a big disappointment. Focus on the process, not on the results.

5

The manager never becomes the champion

The manager is a big influence, but that's not something you need to keep stating. You don't need to take that credit. If a team wins a match, then as the manager you should take a step back and let your team bask in the glory. If you lose, you have to deal with the reporters. That's all part of the manager's role. You are there to protect your team.
In the final analysis it is down to your players – they are the key. That is why the influence of the players as a collective is greater than the influence of the manager. Good managers are more likely to win championships than good players, but the managers themselves never become the champions. I either am not officially an Olympic champion. I don't have a medal, and I think that is how it should be. If I had got one, then the entire support team should have got one. Where do you draw the line? Around the pitch.

A manager's added value lies mainly in putting the team together. A team doesn't necessarily consist of the best players. Eleven Cristiano Ronaldos in one team won't win you a football championship. Holland would not have won the football European Championships in 1988 without its lesser-known players such as Berry van Aerle, Adri van Tiggelen and Jan Wouters. I sometimes heard people say after the Olympics in China that any coach would have won the Olympics with this team. I don't agree. I may not be the only coach who could have done it, but not everyone would for instance have recognised the importance of fitness as I did. Not everyone would have seen that continuing to train on rest days in the Beijing heat was a good idea. Not everyone would have left the reserve keeper behind in Holland.

Not everyone would have analysed all the opponents down to the very last detail. My team of experts helped achieve all that. I want to be clear about that: managing is something you do with your team, your support staff and your experts. I don't know everything. Together, we help each other to keep getting two per cent ahead of the competition, time and time again.

The biggest impact the manager can have is in building the team. Make sure you have diversity within your company or organisation. Take on board that flippant guy who doesn't seem to take anything seriously. We had a physiotherapist like that: always in for a joke, not just an excellent physio with a wealth of experience. Joking with the girls, sometimes about me. He could do that because I was never there. He was often an outlet for the players to vent their feelings after I had once again cracked the whip hard. In other words, a perfect counterweight within the team.

The impact of the coach increases as the crisis and the pressure on an organisation or team increase. A lot of managers don't realise that. "This problem is due to the crisis. I can't do anything about it." They think they have far less influence in times of crisis. No! Your influence is greater when you have to turn a crisis into an opportunity than when you have to go from 'good' to 'better'. My influence after the final we lost in Athens at the 2004 Olympic Games was much greater than after we became world champions in 2006. I could have screamed until I was blue in the face after that World Cup, but nobody would have wanted to change anything. I tried to get the players off the red carpet, away from their gala gowns and premieres (including the one for our own film *Gold*), but I was not always very successful. No-one listened to me. That is one advantage of a crisis: people don't just listen, they are eagerly waiting for you. They want you to take action, to do something, to show leadership. But leadership isn't about slamming your fist on the table and telling people what we're going to do. Leadership is about bringing your team together and asking, "What do you think we should be doing?" And then using all those opinions to draw up a road map.

If you are going to involve your teams in decisions, make sure you ask open questions. I had to learn to do that. In the past I used to explain – no, predict – how we were going to play against Argentina. In China, I asked the players how they thought we should play against Argentina. But do please note: if you are going to ask open questions, it is wise to test the water a bit first. If I was afraid of getting an answer I didn't want, I always checked things out first.

Getting input from your team is very important. My players were able to give a lot of input, especially at the start of a process. There's a good reason why my motto is *Coaching is something you do together*, the title of my first book. I am a fan of servant leadership: letting your team help determine your strategy. Research has been done into how much information people can process in different forms. Then you see that people are best at remembering things they contributed themselves or that they themselves saw or heard. You can use that in your team. As the leader, you set out the broad lines but you let your team fill in the details. Especially if the lines affect individuals and involve the task of a specific person in the team. That lets each individual work out what the coach's strategy means for him or her. I let the players make decisions about alcohol consumption or missing a training session. I took charge of putting together the training schedules, the practice training camps, deciding on how we should play, our tactics and other general matters.

But once I had decided what line we were going to take, I was hard as nails. Get on with it and no more whingeing. You cannot have the entire team continuously having input in the entire process. You are the boss, so from time to time you need to pull rank without apologising, because otherwise they will get confused. People expect a coach or manager to stick to the line they are taking. I have bad experiences of what happens when you don't do that. Sometimes we would be at a training camp and have a free afternoon. Then I would decide on the programme for that afternoon, because if you leave it to the team, three will want to go to the zoo, two to the museum, six will want to lounge by the swimming pool and four would rather go shopping.

Whatever you do, there will always be one or two who don't agree. So don't let them decide. Make the decision yourself; that saves you a lot of aggravation. As a manager, you determine the collective commitment. But once you have decided to go to the zoo, it's up to them whether they watch the polar bears or look at the flamingos first... that's the individual commitment.

The manager role means you are really several coaches at once. One moment I am the driving force, the next I'm the technician, or the bully, and then I'm the psychologist, or the shoulder to cry on. Sometimes you're keeping the players hard at it and at other times you just watch in silence. You need to be prepared to switch tactics if you see your approach isn't working. But that doesn't mean I discard my passion and drive! That's what I heard a manager say recently: "I stick to my guns because otherwise my employees will think I don't believe in my own approach."

> ***Opportunity 8: Let people provide input***
>
> *There is nothing wrong with changing your style as long as you stick to your objectives. You can't spend the entire time walking around with a big whip. Every now and again you need to get closer to your people and let them give input. Once that gets out of hand again, you return to a controlling style. Because input is good, but there are limits. Being involved makes people feel motivated and responsible for things; input can lead to new insights or solutions for the crisis. Input is important both in terms of getting support and in terms of comments. Up to a certain point. You give people an inch and before you know it they've taken a mile. That's when you put on the brakes: this far and no further.*

A lot of people think I had a really open relationship with my players. But I didn't at all. The players would tell the support staff and the physiotherapists all sorts of stuff that they never said to me. I suspect they thought that honesty might cost them their position in the squad. If I speak to the Beijing players now and ask them how things are, I get to hear all their vexations about the training placement schemes arranged by the current national team manager. "I can tell you this now," they say. They could have told me such things at the time, but that just didn't happen. There was a big distance between the manager and the players. I am a fervent perfectionist, which means I do have a tendency to overlook the need for interpersonal communication...
As a player, I also frequently learned things the hard way. But it did teach me a lot. I still remember how as a player I moved to Tilburg. There I was really given a tough time of it by my fellow players Fred Bierens and Frank Leistra. At the time I was really sick to death of it but now I have to thank them. I learned such a lot from their approach. I have even adopted some of it myself... Which doesn't mean I think that it's the only correct method. On the contrary. I know successful coaches who are one of the team. It's just not my style. I did do it every now and again, though, for example when I wrote each of the girls a personal letter just before the start of the Olympics. But such incidents are real exceptions for me, despite the fact that I am an emotional guy. When my mother was dying, she told me I should follow my heart. "Share your uncertainty".
Perhaps I still don't do that enough.

The nice thing about sport at the highest level is that I didn't have to look for a consensus in the typical Dutch way. If the country gets landed with something like a temporary unemployment scheme during an economic crisis, that is simply a consensus-driven compromise for the real solution – changes to our sacking and dismissal rules. Because that is obviously impossible: it would make the trade unions angry, unemployment would rise, you would be destroying human capital and knowledge. Obviously, but you are simply postponing the problem. Take top-level sport. Essentially, every player is a one-person company. And there are no compromises; if you are not up to scratch, you are out of the squad. It's tough, but it benefits the team as a whole.

Misuse the crisis – there is no such thing as a modest coach

Shouldn't we have let the good banks take over the bad banks? Now we are giving support to the banks that didn't perform well and the banks that took fewer risks are suffering as a result. They are facing competition from banks that only survived thanks to government support. That could never happen in top-level sport.

A crisis is the time for change. Whereas you won't be able to make even the slightest amendment when things are going well, you will be able to strike in times of crisis. Changes are accepted under the guise of "It can't get any worse, so we might as well try it." Use this fact – or perhaps even misuse it. Now is the time to resurrect those innovations you had been planning. You have the time and the influence to make it happen. And that can give you just the edge you need when the crisis has passed.

When I started working with the Dutch team in 2001, it was ranked third in the world. There had been arguments during the Olympics in Sydney. That was ideal for me. I said we would be doing things differently. Sulkily, the players agreed. Sometimes I drove the national association's board mad. Video glasses, training camps. "You and your innovations. Why don't you just focus on playing hockey? Stop innovating and start performing." Luckily my players realised that the team development was going well. We didn't always get the right result, but everyone felt they were improving. We were *en route* to getting the top position in the world rankings. We climbed from third to second. Then came the Olympic Games in Athens in 2004. We came second. Not first. I think the board wanted to get rid of me then, but the players expressed their confidence in me. That's why I could continue making changes: the players backed me.

In 2006 we went to the World Cup in Madrid, which we won. That's really when the trouble started; I began to have difficulty getting any new changes past the players. "Marc, this was great. So don't make any more changes now! We're on the way to China!" When I announced that I was already busy with the following changes, I had the players against me for the first time.

Is it false modesty in a coach if he says his impact is not that great? I don't know. Winning often is no coincidence. The football manager Guus Hiddink is the proof of that. If you achieve what he has achieved, it's down to skill. Not luck. If you ask him what his impact is, he is always very reticent. I am too. But look at the facts. I started with the girls' junior team at the Den Bosch club. They had never been national champions, but we got there in my second and third seasons. Then I transferred to the Dutch youth team, who were European champions twice under me. Then I went as a player/coach to Italy, to a club that had just been promoted to the top flight. We became champions. As the manager of the Spanish national team, I oversaw them climbing from the twentieth position in the world rankings to fourth. Under me, the Dutch women's team went from third to first. The most recent trick was at Den Bosch again, avoiding relegation with the men's team last season. There is indeed a certain pattern in all that. Only it sounds so immodest.

Those few CEOs who are able to pull their companies out of a crisis will not be singing their own praises either, even though that might be justified in view of their achievements. All that modesty is also maybe a bit of a Dutch thing. Ask Mr Mourinho at Inter Milan who is the best football manager in the world and you know what answer you will get.

Spain calls and Naomi's chair next to the 'veterans'

How do you become a national manager? This is how it went in my case. In 1996, on the day after Boxing Day, the phone rang. A man spoke in broken English with a Spanish accent. He asked if I wanted to become the manager of Spain's national team.

I had just become an assistant trainer working with Tom van 't Hek for the Dutch women's team. I thought someone was taking the mickey. I asked what they were expecting from me. Would I be able fly to Spain in two days' time? Jokers, I thought. Those friends pulling this joke on me must be rolling around on the floor. But I thought I might as well play along with it. "How did you get my name?" I asked.
It turned out from Gijs van Heumen. Then I thought, "Er, Gijs van Heumen isn't the joking type. He can't possibly be in on the plot." That gave me a bit of food for thought. Afterwards I called Gijs van Heumen straight away and he confirmed the story. He also told me that they had a serious problem in Spain. They had to have me say yes by 1 January 1997 or otherwise they wouldn't get any subsidy money from the Spanish Olympic Committee. There I was, with a contract as an assistant to the Dutch team, with a wife and a three-month-old daughter. Crisis! First I had to know whether my contract with the Dutch team could be dissolved. I phoned Tom van 't Hek and said, "Where are you? I am coming to meet you – I need to discuss something with you."
Tom said at once, "But what about your dream, the Olympic Games? In 1996 you missed the Games in Atlanta as a player because of a broken ankle, now you'll miss them again if you leave us."
Spain was ranked twentieth in the world and only ten countries would be going to the Games. Despite this, Tom said: "You have to do this. It's an opportunity."
He didn't put himself first, and I still appreciate that. We were a good pair; he was an excellent coach and I was a trainer who suited him. We were the perfect match and we had fun together. "In Spain, you must show that you can take final responsibility. Then you'll be able to become the manager of the Dutch national team."
Tom and I got into the car to go to see the chairman of the hockey association, André Bolhuis. We spoke to him between operations in the hospital where he works as a surgeon. He still had his green scrubs on... "What's up?"
I explained about the phone call from Spain. He shook my hand

and said: "Congratulations. One thing: if you do well, make sure you come back after those four years."
I had already said to my wife, Karin, that she shouldn't raise her hopes too much because it probably wouldn't be possible.

Two days later I was sitting in the plane and I signed the contract the very same day. Five days later I held my first training session. Karin had to sell my hockey stick business, rent out the house and look after the little one. She got everything sorted in a couple of weeks. She picked up the baby seat and flew to Spain. The Spanish national women's hockey team didn't have any ambitious targets; they would be quite happy to make the top fifteen in the world because they weren't going to be able to get to the Olympics now anyway. Then I said: "I have three more years. If you can guarantee that the players are prepared to train eight times a week, I'll become your national manager."
We qualified for the Olympic Games. We arrived there like tourists, wearing flip-flops and sun-glasses. "We'll just see what happens. As long as we don't lose too badly."
In Sydney I lost to Tom's Dutch team in the play-off for the third and fourth places. Of course I let them win...

Don't let people automatically move up to higher positions in companies either. Let people prove themselves elsewhere and bring them back when they have proved their worth. Otherwise you will have a lot of people in your company doing jobs for which they used to be the assistant.

Hierarchy is important in times of crisis. Who is going to take on what responsibility? That is why on one of those famous Monday evening sessions at the training camp during the preparations for Beijing, we put the players in a room around a long, U-shaped table. Bouke de Boer was the guest speaker; he is an NLP specialist (neurolinguistic programming). They could sit where they wanted, as long as they did so in hierarchical order. The highest in the hierarchy at one end, the lowest at the other end. That's called group dynamics. Let them decide for themselves who the top dog is. I thought to myself, "We're going to get an argument." Instead something completely different happened, something very surprising. The first six in 'rank' sat down immediately. That was a cut-and-dried thing – the older players. They knew who should sit where, in what order.

The same applied to some extent for the new girls. They quickly went to the other side of the table, giggling. But that middle group. That was the problem. Who had played the most international matches? Who had played the most minutes? Is an attacker more important than a defender? A fascinating performance of doubt, amazement, irritation. What was it all about? Responsibility. If you see yourself as being higher up the hierarchy, it also means you have responsibilities. These players wanted to take on that responsibility. Now they had the chance to demonstrate that in front of the entire group. At a certain point, Naomi van As walked up to the chair at the back, the one closest to the 'veterans'. Responsibility isn't something you are given, you have to take it. The result? Naomi van As started to play better hockey. She felt the responsibility and the team was prepared to give her that responsibility. Look at the hierarchy within companies and organisations. The same applies there. Let the team decide how the responsibilities are to be allocated. I was amazed at the time. I thought I knew these girls, but this session still surprised me. I was expecting arguments and hassles, but the opposite happened. The hierarchy was clear-cut. For everyone. We benefited from that in all the subsequent matches.
That evening, I had to bite my tongue at least ten times because your tendency as a coach – the boss – is to impose your opinion. But the effectiveness lies precisely in letting the team itself decide. Until the point at which you, the boss, can no longer identify with it. In that situation there is only one thing for it: resign.

Thinking freely, relaxing and losing in order to win

If you are to come through a crisis, you need to create a situation in which you can get peace and quiet, think freely and swap ideas with each other. At every Olympic Games since 2000, we had set up our own 'Holland House'. All the players slept in the Olympic Village, but there was always one room that was set up as a shared 'clubhouse', with coffee machines, a laptop with an Internet connection, a sitting area. In short, somewhere to meet up. Papers, magazines, board games.

It was a centre for meeting up and relaxing. There was no requirement to do anything. In Oman we didn't have to do anything either. We didn't have to win; we didn't have to achieve anything. Create a relaxation point in your company, a clubhouse, somewhere to meet up. The reflex reaction is often: "It's a crisis, so we have to work even harder". But if you hit your shot over the top of the goal, what's the point of hitting the ball harder? You only make it go faster over the net – you still haven't scored. So it's all very well dealing with the crisis by working even harder, but it would be better to place that shot between the posts.
You could say it's all very well saying this, because you won't get anywhere if you don't put the effort in. If you are training you aren't winning matches. But training does help you to be better for the next match. And I repeat: you never learn any new tricks from the matches.

Winning is more important than taking part. That was the players' motto. I thought it was an original statement, but also a dangerous one. Because then you are focusing on the target, and that's not good. We don't have one hundred per cent control over winning or losing a match. Think about the influence of the opponent: "I got my shirt pulled just when I was about to score".
The referees: "What a ridiculous decision. This way we'll never win."
The pitch: "What a terrible pitch! That will cause us more problems than the opponent..."
The weather: "You can't play hockey in this heat!"
Or a company that says: "Oh dear, credit crisis, no-one will buy my product now..."

As a manager, I do think it's important to define a joint target, a so-called 'dream target'. Something you are allowed to get: winning the Olympics. But then it should disappear to the background. Keeping that target in mind, I want to get on with the process and define the performance objectives. What do we want to achieve, step by step? What does that mean for the personal development plans of the individual players? What do we want to change in our tactics? What innovations are we going to implement? Because those are all things you have complete control over. The result is the consequence of a process.

As a manager, you focus on the process. The result follows automatically. If you focus on the result (which you don't have full control over) you will get stuck. I see far too much focus in companies on the result, on shareholder value, on maximising profits, on targets, on bonuses. What do you then get? Stress, because those are things you don't have complete control over. And then people blame each other for the failures. Or they say it's due to the credit crisis: "That's why I can't perform well." Then people are not focusing on their own actions but on factors that are stopping them from acting. I know what I'm talking about, as a former national team manager of the European, World and Olympic champions. It's not about the scoreboard, because the scoreboard shows the result. By that time you are too late.
Statistics measure the process. That's what it's all about. Even losing can be a means to winning.

One of the mistakes we made during the 2004 Olympics in Athens is that we didn't keep our focus. We went on trips on the rest days during the tournament. That broke the flow. Players were lying on the beach. "Look, those hockey players are drinking beer." That wasn't the case; they were sitting at the same table as their boyfriends, who were drinking beer. But all those things did cause irritation. We didn't let that happen in China. We continued training every single day. Nobody asked whether they could go to the Great Wall of China. No parents, no boyfriends. That was on their own request. We were there with one mission: to win. Each successive match. Everything else had to contribute to that process.

In Athens in 2004, we were already busy with the festivities at the end – the result – when we still had to play the final against Germany. The association approached me asking me to cooperate with a joint reception with the players who had won gold for the Dutch team twenty years earlier in Los Angeles. We would be winning gold at the Olympic Games for the second time in our history.

The Dutch Olympic Committee had already gone through the entire protocol with us: what time we had to be where with our gold medals. The press weren't asking us whether we were going to beat Germany, they were asking us how: "Just like in the pool match, I suppose, when you smashed them 5-1?"
I can still remember how the thought flashed through my mind during the match that it was a real shame that all those former international players had now come to Athens for nothing. That defeat, the biggest sporting crisis in my life, taught me to focus on the process and not the result. In China I cut short all requests for parties before the final: "You figure it out, I don't want to hear anything about it."
I had also agreed with the team manager Sandra le Poole that we wouldn't respond to anything else beforehand. She kept everything out of the way for me. Perhaps that is the advantage of losing. Then you have a better idea of how to win and what you need to avoid to get there. I lost the World Cup final in 2002 and the Olympic final in 2004. My friend and the former keeper for the men's hockey team, Ronald Jansen, told me then: "Marc, you have to lose two finals first before you can win one..."

Another good example of focus, expressed in practical rules? The players agreed amongst themselves that as of 1 March 2008 everything would be centred on the Games. They put their studies on hold, resigned from their jobs. The issue of alcohol came up. "Not a drop" was the agreement. But one player, Maartje

Goderie, said she used to go out for a meal once a month with her boyfriend and she really liked to have one glass of wine then with the meal. Then they agreed that one glass a month was the absolute limit. The funny thing was that somehow this got into the media and all those journalists thought I had imposed that rule on the players. After we'd explained it three times we gave up and left it. Anyway, it was an initiative of the players. So if you want introduce more focus into your company or organisation, it also means you will have to give up some things.

If you are in a process, you need to maintain a very tight focus. You mustn't have anything else bothering you. I have never really said this publicly but my wife Karin understands this really well. If I was coaching then I was coaching and so she wouldn't phone me. She never asked whether I could phone her once in a while. She knew what I was doing. It is important that the people around you understand your flow and don't break it. Karin is my best coach. She never complained whenever I went away again for weeks on end, although I know for certain she wasn't always happy about it. "Good luck," she would say, "and don't let them get to you".

I remember I was seething after the maker of the documentary film *Gold* had invited me to see the film before it was shown in cinemas. The film concentrated entirely on our World Cup win in 2006; the cameras had followed us around for a whole year. I thought it was a completely stupid film, an emotional melodrama with nothing but lost matches in the run-up, which didn't match the real situation at all. I rushed through the film as the bad guy who spent his whole time carping and swearing. But the documentary maker was not a coach. He looks at things as a filmmaker and he wants to achieve a certain effect: from the doldrums to the ultimate victory. I had had quite enough of it and told the association that I didn't want to attend the film's première. Then I showed the film to Karin, my wife. She thought it was great. She saw what the filmmakers were trying to do. So we went to the premiere together.

No sports psychologists, but secretly...

In the end we were the only country in Beijing not to have a sports psychologist. The Dutch Olympic Committee felt, and still feels, that sports psychologists should have done their job before a major tournament. But Rico Schuijers was in China, of course. No-one knew that apart from the team. And I made use of his presence and expertise there on location. Bart Veldkamp, the Olympic speed skating champion, was in China filming brief items for the Dutch sports programme Studio Sport.

In one of those items he expressed his surprise that Holland hadn't brought any mental coaches. Now I can reveal that Bart was wrong... It is true that Rico wasn't in the Olympic Village but we could contact him easily if we needed him. A tournament is hard going mentally as well. During the preparations we benefited a lot from his approach. We didn't want to run the risk in China of overlooking something because we didn't have him.

If I had to put the physical, mental, tactical and technical aspects of the preparation for an Olympic tournament in order of importance, I would say the physical aspect is the most important, followed by mental attitude. Tactics and technique come after that. So shouldn't the Dutch Olympic Committee allow us to have a specialist in our team for that mental aspect, which I estimate at thirty per cent of the total? We solved that problem ourselves. Say something goes wrong during the tournament. If it's physical, we have doctors. If it's tactical, we have video analyses and so on. You can't change much in a few days if it's technical. But if it's psychological, a mental attitude thing, you can pull someone right out of the dumps in a few minutes and make sure they regain their focus. That's why I think someone like that belongs on your support team. We had no less than six doctors during the Olympic Games. They were sitting there waiting for something to happen. But they could have made that four plus two mental coaches. I chose to do it my way.

In the past, when I was a young trainer, I wouldn't have had the courage to do that; I wanted to be liked. But later on I thought it was much more important for them to say after a tournament that I was a good coach. I no longer needed to be liked. It just happens to be the case that you always have a love-hate relationship with players and board members. One minute they are pleased with you, the next minute you are a bastard. I see that other coaches often have difficulty with this. I see that managers don't have the courage to make hard decisions because they want to be liked. Often, I would only receive acknowledgement for my work six months after the event.

I will be honest with you – of course I am looking for that acknowledgement. Everyone needs that.

It is often the case that you will only receive acknowledgement for changes, reorganisations or innovations much later. There is always resistance in the beginning. Why? You are pushing back the frontiers. People feel it's unnecessary. "Surely it's not going that badly? Stop griping."
The second thing you'll encounter are the teething problems. Little problems at the start. You modify something, you see if it works and you go further. You'll get resistance there too: "See, it's not working. What did I tell you?"
It may only start working properly later and it's only after that that you may get a compliment. So as a coach, a manager, you have to assume it will take months before the process has got to that stage. You won't get any compliments during the process, so be prepared for that. Sometimes I have even exploited my 'role as bastard'. I pushed things in that direction. Then I was the team's common enemy, as it were. Rinus Michels, the former Dutch national football coach, used to do that as well. He used to organise general vendettas against the bigwigs. Sometimes I have driven players so hard that they had to throw up. "Ridiculous," they thought. On occasion they even said to me: "Marc, you'd better enjoy this World Cup because it's going to be your last as national coach!"
They were furious. When I asked them years later what they thought of the approach, they referred to a hard day's training as

a peak. “You made us push back the frontiers then. That’s when we became stronger as a team.”
As a coach you are not there to be liked. You are there to make the team better. In the end the players should respect you, you should be able to demand things from them. And they should trust you, be able to trust you. That’s a question of using your intuition. It’s fine to be a bastard every now and again, but not all the time. It’s okay to want to be liked sometimes, but not all the time. That is not good. You won’t make any progress that way. Situational leadership? Directive leadership? Laissez faire? Self-management? I think what you really need to do is use several different styles.

Opportunity 9: Coach? Get yourself a coach

You don’t have a good overview when you are in the middle of a crisis. Who coaches the coach? Who manages the manager? Other people can provide the overview. So make sure you have one or two reliable, professional coaches around. Coaches who know you and understand what kind of a crisis you are in. So make use of their wise advice. There’s nobody more opinionated than coaches and managers...

I already mentioned my most important coach: my wife. I also have a select group of people who I consider as my coaches. My support team, Rico Schuijers (at that time the Dutch national team’s mental coach), Jan Albers (then the team manager, now chairman of the association), Ties Kruize (former international and an association board member), Marjolein Bolhuis (ditto), André Bolhuis (former chairman of the hockey association) and Sandra le Poole (the general manager for the Dutch national team in the two years leading up to Beijing). When you are in the middle of a crisis, you don’t actually notice it much yourself, you are not aware of it. You just feel the disadvantages, the trouble. That’s when it’s important to have people around you who can coach you. I have always been very careful in choosing my 'coaches', but I've always been open to the suggestions the people I choose make. As a young and inexperienced coach I wasn't able to take a bird's eye view and evaluate my own coaching. So I wasn't able to call myself to order. Who coaches the coach? That's a matter of conscience for many a businessman, manager or director. The answer to that question determines whether you will have to drag yourself through a crisis or whether there are people around you who can help you. Or even simply make you aware that you are in a crisis. There is one coach I have not mentioned yet: my team. Of course, my players were continuously coaching me – without realising it. These days, in the talks I give to companies and organisations around the country, I try to be the coach of managers, executive boards, employees and team leaders. I provide them with the bird's eye view. I get them thinking outside the box.

The Lammers secret, tunnels and fiddling about in the corner

My secret? Constant perfectionism using a step-by-step approach. Everything has to be perfect, but I'm quite okay getting there with fifty steps of two per cent. That is the contradiction that eventually made my approach so successful. Most perfectionists don't have the patience. Me neither, but I had a support team with me who helped me to stay patient. That approach resulted in a team of players who were able to make the right choices themselves. Independently of me. In the Olympic final in Beijing, I heard my Chinese colleague yelling at his players because they expected him to tell them what they had to do. But he was inaudible because the spectators in the stadium were making such a racket that you could forget hearing or seeing anything. I only discussed things with my players on the bench. I hardly called out anything from the sidelines that was crucial for tactics. I was more cheering them on. They took their own decisions. That gave me real satisfaction. I had put that team of players together like pieces of a puzzle so that everyone benefited. I had been allowed to take the best players and make them into the best team. I realised this when it got to 2-0 in the final. At that score I saw Naomi van As running with the ball towards the corner of the pitch and just fiddling about with it. She knew she shouldn't go take on an opponent and try to get back in the circle for a chance for 3-0. She knew she should keep dribbling in order to retain possession of the ball and run the clock down. That was something I was proud of; that the players understood the match like that. But in the right perspective; top-level sport means you sweat for five thousand hours in order to enjoy it for ten minutes. Top-level sport is fun? No way. It's only nice when you've won. Getting there is not always so pleasant. My wife Karin said to me after I quit as national team coach: "You never really enjoyed your work." I think she was right. Although I do look back on that period now with considerable pleasure.

Team leaders, managers and businessmen in times of crisis need to understand that they will not be getting too much fulfilment for a while.

That will only come much later. Of course it's okay to enjoy your minor success stories. A quick celebration and then on to the next round. Real fulfilment – that's something for after the crisis. As a manager you are sometimes in a tunnel, just like in top-level sport; cut off from the outside world, stuck in your own organisation and strategy. I sat in my personal tunnel for four years. If you can't see the end of the tunnel as a manager, make sure you make your tunnel shorter. Make sure you modify your objectives. Because nobody gets through a tunnel without daylight at the other end.

Looking at it from the opposite perspective, you can also create a tunnel. If you're a company making a plan for the next four years, make sure you also have employment contracts for four years. Not necessarily permanent contracts, so that you can still make changes. And give people the space to make a switch. The employment contracts could be for 50 months; the employee then has two months paid leave to find a new job. That can sometimes give people the time to relax. The players in the Dutch team suddenly started to make huge improvements when we started measuring relaxation. If I look at myself, I was totally exhausted after four years. I was pleased I could get my breath back and go off and do other things. That stimulates you again, so that you automatically feel like getting on with something fanatically again.

Perhaps I will stay in the hockey world in addition to my work as a business consultant and coach. I am really enjoying my time as performance manager for Den Bosch. But I've never been in charge of the Dutch men's hockey eleven. I'm not saying I would never want to take on a challenge like that. I'm also attracted by the world of professional football. There, too, I see opportunities for my performance management. I don't think I can put it more neutrally than that...

I have now come out of my tunnel as hockey coach. I am standing out in the open. It is true I helped stop Den Bosch from getting relegated from the men's first division at the end of the 2008-2009 season, but I only did that because I knew how short the tunnel was: four weeks.

I am enjoying the light and the nature around me. I have no idea what my next tunnel will be. I do know for certain that there will come a time when I will want to get back to my old level. I will get the itch again – success is addictive. But I was sitting at home crying during the last two summers before the Games in China. Those were the times when I swore I would never start something like this again. The sacrifice did get to be too much sometimes. There was my wife with the kids in France on holiday. I was at home, just back from a training camp. The phone rang. My daughter sobbing on the line. "Dad, are you going to get divorced?"
When I asked where she got that idea, she said, "The children here at the camp site say it means your parents are going to get divorced if your dad doesn't come with you on holiday."
Then I caught the next plane to join them, even though I only had four days off. I arrived on the Tuesday and on the Friday we were due to all drive back to Holland. As soon as I had arrived, my wife said, "I've had enough of this, I want to go home."
We stayed there that evening; I had a couple of beers with friends

and was well and truly sick during the night. From the stress, the pressure. The next morning I drove home with my family. There was nothing wrong with me any more.

Of course I heard and saw stories in the media and from people around me, who basically said I had gone nuts. On rest days during the Olympics we were on the training pitch even though it was 35 degrees. Other teams were enjoying the rest, but not us. We kept to our rhythm and trained for ninety minutes. Mind you, China were training on the pitch next to us and they trained twice as long on rest days. They were even doing sprints on rest days, without sticks or balls. I didn't do that. Our training sessions always concentrated on what was needed for the match and were no longer focusing on technique and endurance. I'm not claiming there's only one right way, but I will point out that the two finalists kept on working while the others were lounging by the swimming pool. I had learned from Athens 2004 that a rest day can put you out of your flow.

You often hear cyclists in the Tour de France say that too. They take their bikes on a rest day as well and do a round trip of a hundred kilometres. It is very important to rest; training hard means resting hard too. And we did that every day too.

Organisations and companies need to keep moving too in times of crisis, but they still need to focus on what the market is demanding. Don't be too short-sighted in judging that. If the past few years were a crisis in a positive sense as you tried to get all the work finished, make sure you take some rest when demand drops off. As a businessman or manager in a crisis period you might think you are just about to play the Olympic final and you need a big effort with all hands on deck. But perhaps your Olympics are already over and you already put in everything you had over the past few years. In fact, the intensity of the training schedules for the Dutch team players was reduced dramatically after the Olympics, precisely so that it could be built up again over the next four years.

This Dutch women's hockey team has such a surplus of talent that I am prepared to make the prediction that they will be world champions in 2010 and Olympic champions again in 2012. If they don't have any arguments, at any rate. Younger players are fitting in well. We had the youngest players at the Games in China: Liedewij Welten and Eva de Goede, both 17. We also had another three who were under twenty and about eight aged 22 or 23. The underlying strategy of 'always change a winning team' has given them a leading edge that will be there for years yet. When I started as the national team coach I also held a lot of training sessions for national junior teams – the Under 16s and the Under 18s. I had more than enough on my hands with the Dutch women's team but I saw the advantage of getting to know the next generation. That would help me to fit young players in more easily. That was when the idea of placement schemes for young players started. Taking part in a training camp with the Dutch national team, just to get a flavour of the atmosphere, show what you can do at the highest level. Afterwards those players went back to their own teams.

There is a lot of talent walking around in companies too: young people you should let try out another job. If you are looking for a manager, you place an advert or get hold of a recruitment agency. Whereas the best managers may actually already be in your company, only they have never had the chance to prove themselves. I saw Eva de Goede in the Under 16s junior team. She was fifteen at the time. At her club she didn't even play in the women's first team, she played in the juniors' first team. When she was 16, I invited her to a Dutch national team training camp. "Ridiculous," they said, "that girl doesn't even play in the first team for her club." A year later she went with us to China and played a fantastic tournament. Don't let people get automatic promotions; encourage them to prove themselves elsewhere. Eva started to play better for her club as well after she had been on that training camp with the Dutch national team.

6

Make sure you get into a flow

The optimum mental condition for achieving is sometimes called the 'flow'. It is part of the positive psychology of the American Mihaly Csikszentmihalyi. You are fully motivated and concentrated, fully involved in what you are doing, all your energy is going into your one goal and – most importantly – you are tasting success and gaining self-confidence. Knowing that, it was clear to me: I had to find out how to get my players into a flow. But how? Because what typifies a flow is that you don't know that you're in one and the moment you become aware of it, the flow immediately disappears. In 2000, I was in a flow with the Olympic team in Spain. Until a journalist said to my players, "If you win one more match you'll be playing in the final..." We promptly lost to New Zealand, on paper the weakest opponent. I had also already experienced various periods of flow with the Dutch national team. The World Cup in Madrid, for example. But how do you get into that flow? By aiming for the right balance between challenges and objectives on the one hand, and between skills and experience on the other.

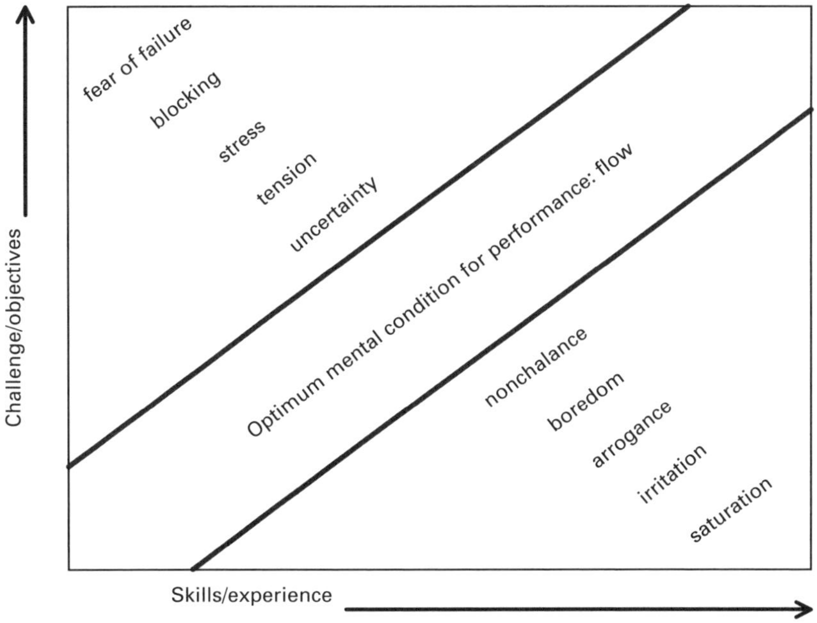

The central diagonal area in the diagram above is the flow area: a good balance between challenges and skills.
If you don't have sufficient skills yet and the challenges and targets set are very high, you'll end up in the area with pressure and fear of failure. Young players who were still a bit short on skills and had hardly any experience were expected to win an Olympic medal. They soon came to me saying, "I find it a bit scary."
On the other hand, there were players who had played in more than a hundred international matches, who had been at the Games in Athens and who were not really challenged by the training sessions. They were bored and satiated. "Oh no, not that exercise again!"
So my job was to enhance the skills and reduce the level of challenges for the players who were under pressure or were afraid of failure. And at the same time, the players who were bored and satiated were given more challenges and fewer standard exercises. Fatima Moreira de Melo was one of those experienced players who had to be challenged now and then.

I told her about a magnificent trick that I had seen a Spanish player use on TV. She lifted the ball, tapped it in one direction and then – while the ball was still in the air – tapped it the opposite way. It was a marvellous move for dribbling past someone. I had made the whole story up... but I didn't tell her that. Fatima Moreira de Melo is the kind of woman who won't rest until she can do it too. And so she started messing about with the idea. Weeks later, she called me over. "Marc – I can do it!" I looked at her, but had no idea what she was going on about. Then she did it: lifted the ball and, while it was still in the air, hit it to the left then to the right and off she went. She turned around, filled with pride. "And? How did you like that?"

I said, "I've never seen anything like that before."

"Yes, you have," she said. "It's that move by the Spanish player that you told me about a while back."

At that point, I had to confess to her that I had made up that move myself, just to challenge her. I'd given her a difficult task to make her sharp and to keep her from dropping off. I think she appreciated it (although she called me a bastard at the time). And I simply had to admire her skill once again.

You can compare this with a crisis in a company or organisation. If you keep hammering on about the results, young and inexperienced people will get stressed and be afraid of failure. That's when the level of challenges should be reduced. Old hands should really assert themselves in situations of crisis. That's when the level of challenges should be raised. If you have experienced a crisis before, you are better equipped for dealing with the current one. Make sure the right people bear the responsibility: the ones with the most skills and experience.

People who are in a flow seem to be distracted from the rest of the World. You can see that they're in a trance, totally absorbed in what they're doing. Players who are complaining about the referee are not in a flow. They are not focusing on their own actions, but are getting caught up in peripheral activities. It has a lot to do with concentration and focus. The flow can also be seen in moments when you are performing at your highest level. In sports, people often talk about 'peaking at the right moment'.

This flow is a mental peak. It may just last for a few minutes, or can persist for weeks – for an entire tournament. It's the realisation that you can't lose. Dennis Menchov, the leader of the Rabobank cycling team, won the Tour of Italy in 2009, when he was in a flow. But there was no flow during the Tour de France. He sank without a trace.

Sometimes I could see a player doing things during a training session that made me think: "I wish she'd do that during a match."
Sometimes the circumstances are ideal, yet you can see players struggling with themselves on the pitch. You know what the players are capable of: they show it time and again during the training sessions. A flow lets everyone do the best they can. If you're able to channel that and reserve it for an Olympic tournament, you'll win gold. So it was extremely important for me to get those girls into a flow. That's why I wanted to know everything about the subject. You could also compare it to the 'trance' that high jumpers get into. In their mind they are already jumping over the bar; they visualise their jump, they shut themselves off from the outside world, they persuade themselves to fly for just a moment.

As a team's manager, you're often part of the flow of your team. You may not be not aware of it, but everything suddenly starts working. Becoming aware of it means the end of the flow. Flow just happens to you: it's not something you can get into just like that. I experienced it in China. Everything went smoothly; you could say that I was at my peak. Team discussions went perfectly, I discovered things in the analyses that were very valuable for the next match, everything went okay, everything worked. If at that moment I had thought, "Hey, wait a minute – am I in a flow?" then I would have been out of it again.
I was in the fear-of-failure area myself too. I told myself that I had

to become an Olympic champion. “Surely I’ll be able to do it this time? As long as I don’t really blow it.” I had to get rid of all those performance targets. I doubted whether I was good enough. Women often do that too. They’re quick to say, “I can’t do this, I can’t do that,” when they can in fact do it very well. The opposite goes for men: They say, “I can do that” and it then turns out that they can’t.

I had to persuade myself to enjoy the match that we had played and work on the next one. I had to get that final target out of my head in order to prevent the pressure from building up too high. It’s the difference between demanding from yourself that you win all the matches, or that you play well next match. The target is different, but the result is the same.

If you want another nice visual example of a team in a flow, have a look at the Dutch team, lined up for the Olympic final, listening to the national anthem. The TV camera went along the line and you could tell by the girls’ faces that they were in just the right state of mind. In fact, that wink from Maartje Goderie was the confirmation: “I’m in a flow.”

The ‘crisis flow’, Ageeth the Tormentor and Maartje the Marker

Realising that you’re in a flow means the end of the flow. That’s the big risk: it can all be over in a second. How can you avoid that? By continuously looking for a balance between challenges and skills. When we had to play against Italy, I knew what the players were thinking: “We can beat that lot with our hands tied behind our backs.”

So I showed them twenty-five goals scored by Italy before that game. Okay, those were all the goals that they had scored over the last few years, but I didn’t tell them that. So I bolstered the level of the challenge at moments when boredom threatened to strike.

A businessman should dare to look at his company in that way, try to approach a crisis in that way. A balance between challenges and skills. If everything within the organisation is focused on surviving the crisis, you won't survive, because you're aloof from the flow. Team members who were afraid they would not be selected for the Dutch team for the Olympic Games were indeed not selected. The players who concentrated on the next match or training session and who showed what they could do were the ones who went to Beijing.

Managers who focus during a time of crisis on the question of whether they are going to be fired will be fired. Others, who continue to focus on improving the execution of their tasks, will often stay. Try to find a balance between performance targets and skills, even in times of crisis. If you have time left, train people. If you're on the edge of bankruptcy, use every sales trick you can think of – discounts, savings stamps, free delivery, offers, sales... But try to find the right balance and handle challenges in a positive way.

Having a sale when there's no need to do so will make your employees lazy. Teaching people new skills when customers are about to leave your company will ruin your business. Recently I saw a booklet with an intriguing cover: the front of a shop with a small sign behind the window: 'Closed for customer orientation training'. They were certainly not in a flow there! Make an inventory of the challenges that the crisis is making you face. Make an inventory of the associated performance targets. Look at the experience and skills within your company and create a balance. Win the next match. Keep doing that and eventually you will win the gold medal.

You don't make mistakes when you're in a flow, so pointing out the mistakes won't get you into the flow.

Winning gold without a flow seems impossible to me. I spoke to the German team after the 2004 Olympic final, in which they beat us. "We were in a flow, we knew beforehand that we would play well. The final? It seemed like it only lasted a few minutes. Everything went naturally, we just did everything right."

We came second there. And winners of the silver medal always say, "We were in a flow. Until the final..."

I have to admit now that our flow had already gone during the semi-final. We only won it on penalties. There was too much emotion, too much relief. The euphoria afterwards was intense; we actually celebrated the best possible result. It seemed as if we had already reached our target.

Then came the final and we were poor. We no longer had the energy to play.

Intimidation, irritation, reactions: these are all things that your opponent can use to get you out of your flow. But you will be your own worst enemy too, if you don't look out. During the preparations for China, we went on a training tour to Argentina. We were in a hotel that temporarily had no phone or Internet. Less than a day later, the players said to each other and to me, "It's so peaceful! Isn't that great?" That led me to ask the team what we were going to do with telephones and Internet in Beijing. "Let's not take phones with us to Beijing." We were one of the few teams at the tournament without mobile phones. No Internet, except at our own 'Holland House' and we made agreements about the hours that the Internet would be available. And that worked out very well. One day before the final of the European Championships in Manchester, we had received that message I mentioned before, that the team wanted to start legal proceedings against the hockey association about their image rights. I said that I definitely didn't want things like that to happen any more.

It's difficult to get your opponent out of their flow. Ageeth Boomgaard in particular was really good at it: tormenting opponents, driving them mad, frustrating them. We didn't make any agreements about that; some experienced players don't even need explaining. I tried it once during half time against Argentina by saying to their star player Aymar, "I've never seen you play so well." You just hoped that it would get her out of her flow. I have no idea whether it helped for the second half of that match.

But it did during the Olympic final in China. We were in a flow, but what about them? The home team, in the final, one match away from eternal fame in their own country! The Chinese culture (and therefore the Chinese hockey team too) are totally structured. If they could play the final within their own structure, we would lose. We knew that from our 'China week' that we had organised in May 2008.

We focused on China exclusively for an entire week, as I knew that they would do well as the home country. Their flow was all about structure.
And so what did we do? We messed up that structure. During the final we changed systems several times; we played with four up front for a while, followed by ten minutes with just the one centre forward. We had practised this specifically during training games, deliberately targeting China.
It drove them crazy. Their team's manager was screaming like mad, but the stadium was filled with thousands of Chinese, each one of them making enough of a racket for ten. Doubts rose in the Chinese team. They didn't know where they ought to be. They saw their manager gesturing frantically, but they weren't able to understand him. There goes your flow.
Before that, we had also managed to break Argentina's flow. I knew that Argentina play well if their star player Aymar is on form. So I had no less than three players take up position in Aymar's zone to keep her quiet. Maartje Goderie's teasing and tormenting went right to the limit. At one point Aymar was replaced by another player and Maartje walked with her all the way to the side of the pitch, as if marking her even then. She looked at Aymar, smiling. Aymar got so annoyed that she couldn't hit a single ball right any more. And her team went down with her.

Map, Dubai, the girls are seeing f(l)ame

The media often get you out of the flow. If your team is doing well, they can't exactly deny it. But if something goes wrong, the media always manage to make things worse than they are. They sometimes tempted me to say the wrong things in interviews too. Without realising it, I put so much pressure on my players that my media appearances made my own team lose their flow. The media just focus on the scoreboard, the performance target, and so it's only natural that the unfair expectations get the players out of their rhythm.

I made very clear internal agreements with the hockey association about how I wanted to handle this in China. "You can say whatever you like and you can tell those players whatever you think, but you're *not* going to talk about winning or losing. You don't have to come onto the pitch after the matches either. Or only the chairman, at any rate."
And everyone stuck to these agreements.
Create your own flow. At the moment you become aware of your flow, it will be gone.

Opportunity 10: Create a flow in your own organisation

Managers, directors, coaches: create a flow in your own organisation. Reserve time, create space to think. Do you know the tale of the lumberjack who was having trouble chopping down a tree? He was sweating buckets. A passer-by gave him a hint and told him to sharpen his axe. "I ain't got no time for that," said the lumberjack and he went on slaving away. In my opinion, people have too much of a tendency to keep on chopping in times of crisis. Sharpen your axe! A sharp axe will get you into a flow and will fell the tree.

Of course, we hadn't had to make changes to the team for quite a while. Not since 2006. We became world champions, we won the Champions Trophy, it was all positive, nothing had to be changed. Until we lost the European Championship final. That was when we had to start pruning again if we were to play better in Beijing.
This applies to companies too. They may not have had to

economise and reduce costs for years. When a crisis comes along, you can see that them reviewing the situation too. A crisis forces you to have take close look at what you've done and what you're doing.

In Oman, we had set out our standards and values for the preparations for Beijing. The only thing we hadn't done was put them on paper. We only made a report of them. But the report wasn't half as decisive as the agreements that we had made.

So I decided to map out the information. Literally. Including routes, pitfalls, setbacks, risks, challenges, strong points and weak points of the team. We used it for a team-building session. The girls were split up into five groups; each group got a sheet of paper and everyone could draw their own personal route to Beijing. All symbols on the map were explained – mountains, lighthouses, towns, bridges, you name it. Then all the groups returned and explained their own map to the others. We had those five maps combined into a single complete map: *The Road to F(l)ame.*
(You can find the map in the photo pages in the centre of this book.)

During the Olympic Games we had a life-sized version of this map in our own Holland House, the 'living room' where we gathered for team meetings and sociability. At first our players giggled at it. But gradually you could see players reminding each other of the agreements made in Oman, using the map. Standards and values were referred to, and players spoke to each other about them. Of course, the map was also the source of a lot of fun. "Oh no, you're in the Bay of Whinges again," I once heard a player call out. Or "Stop it now, all of you, and get out of the Ocean of Gossiping!" The map also shows how hard we trained in the 'Desert of Sweat' in 'Do Bay' (sounds like *Dubai* in Dutch). We had to watch out for the 'Media Swamp'. My own contribution to the map also included the 'Province of Sixteen Million Coaches' (i.e. the whole Netherlands). The map was the guarantee for the agreements that we had made. The map made sure that problems and pitfalls could be identified. In fact, they are the ifs and don'ts of the team. When you look back on it, it's nothing but risk management. We made an overview of all the risks, albeit in a unique way. That map was a prime example of the team's creativity. You could see it on the pitch too; creativity was an important factor in this team. After we won the final, we hung the big map up in the 'Holland Heineken House'. They had to cordon off the spot with cones and tape later on because so many people were pushing past each other just to have a look at that map.

And as you can see on the map, 'Champagne Bay' is beyond Beijing...
If you were to ask the players now whether that map helped them, they'll say that it didn't do a great deal. But without us realising it, that map kept us on the right track. This map gave me peace of mind as the team's manager. The process had been mapped out.

Ultimately, I had made that map because of my own fears. Fear of losing, fear of coming second again, fear of failing. That applied to my team too. After winning two matches during the Olympic tournament, fear struck there too: will we manage to win? Not the younger girls, not so much the older players either, but the group in between. They had started to have doubts. I sat down with them. They thought they were going to be given a video analysis. But no, we were going to talk. I addressed them personally. I asked, "What's wrong with you all?"
The emotional outpouring was huge. It was, after Oman, the second moment of change. Several of players started crying. "The whole thing seems so scary to me."
The younger players were more like: "Now that we're here, who cares? This is fun, isn't it?"
The map – *The Road to F(l)ame* – does not permit the 'uncertainty' aspect either. It had not been mentioned. As the team's manager, I thought that we would no longer be troubled by un-

certainty after we'd won two matches comfortably. We played better after that group discussion. Think of that wonderful match against the Argentineans. In my opinion, that is the most beautiful hockey match that I've ever coached in my entire life.

The first item at the top of the map had initially said *Winning is more important than taking part*. Yet those girls preferred *The Road to F(l)ame*. I thought it focused too much on 'fame'. It gave me an uncomfortable feeling, we should not have been thinking of that yet. The 'fame' would only come at the end. But the 'flame' was there too. We had to go through fire and water for each other to reach that fame in the end.

They went for the Olympic flame, at that camp fire in Oman. That was where the foundations were laid.
I wonder if it would be possible to create such a map with a men's team. Did you notice that the map didn't show any opponents? It did not show a penalty corner. No smooth passes anywhere. Or a foul. I think that men would have focused more on those technical, analytical details. And they do sometimes say that I'm a team manager who only thinks about technique and statistics. But this map is pure emotion. Not quantifiable. But it was a perfect way of making sure that the team became 'unconsciously skilled'.

Morning meetings, circles and overtime

A crisis is not a flow, by definition. Your own flow is broken if your actions and tasks are disrupted. A crisis involves just that kind of disruption. So if you adapt your actions and tasks during a crisis, it may be possible for you to get into the right flow again. For the average person, the most effective period is between three and five hours after waking up. But for a lot of people those are also the hours that they are trying to work and are continuously being interrupted by e-mails, phone calls, colleagues, etc. I sometimes wonder why companies don't start working from seven in the morning to three in the afternoon. You can use the first couple of hours for yourself, because nobody calls or sends you e-mail before nine. And after that you can focus entirely on your customer, your team, your task, in your most effective hours. Studies show that important matters are hardly handled after three in the afternoon. So let your secretary handle phone calls from three to five and your company's effectiveness will increase enormously, with people working from seven in the morning until five in the afternoon. If you, given your role as a manager, were to start working at six a.m. you'd have an hour to empty your mailbox, after which you'd be ready to deal with your 'players' at seven. I would say that overtime only really works when it's glued on first in the mornings. That lets you avoid the traffic-jam crisis and you'll have more quality time in return at home, as you'll be able to pick up the kids from school. You'll be more able to join in the rhythm of your family.

We did that with the Dutch team too. We stopped holding meetings with the technical staff at night, after training sessions. It had a lot of disadvantages. You're tired. You're taking all the emotions with you to the meetings and there's no fixed end. Net result? We were discussing items well into the night. Being the national team's manager, I then went to bed with all that misery and couldn't sleep a wink. We decided to do it the other way round. The coaching staff started working one hour earlier in the morning than the players, then later on even an hour and a half earlier. First we ran for half an hour and then we held a one-hour meeting. It was impossible to hold longer meetings, since we had to work with the team afterwards. We noticed that the discussions became shorter and less emotional; we had literally been able to 'sleep on' problems. In short, we became more effective. A director recently told me that he had stopped holding weekly board meetings with his three other members of the board. They call each other every day at 7:30 am from their cars. A conference call during which they have each other on the line. Current matters are discussed, problems exchanged and after that everyone is updated for a day. In the end they only needed to meet up in person once a month.

To create a flow, you need to know which aspects you can influence and which you can't. You can not exert any influence directly on winning or losing. But you can affect the process. I went through all the 'circles of influence' to see if I could affect them from my role as the team's manager and if so, by how much.

1. You do have a lot of influence on yourself and your task (player, guide, manager).
2. You have an influence on the team.
3. Parents, friends, the board of the hockey association… you don't have so much influence there.
4. Other hockey players, the 'sector', opponents, referees, the spectators: you have hardly any influence on them.
5. You have little or no influence on the media, the Internet or the Dutch people.
6. On the circumstances (pitch, weather, etc.), you have no influence at all.
7. And then the outermost circle: the consequence of the result, 'the world'.

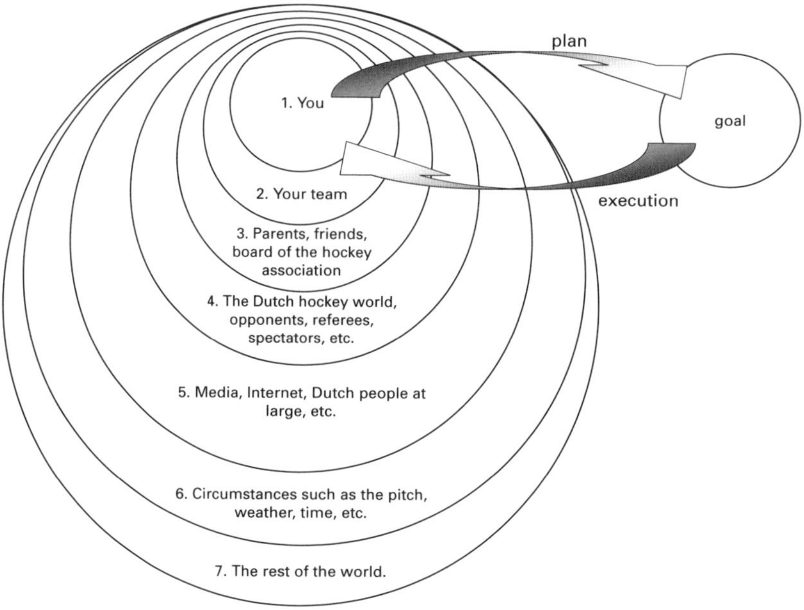

Circles of influence

During the European Championships in Manchester in 2007, we were nowhere near being in our flow. All kinds of sideline activities kept us occupied there. Parents who were ringing up to say, "My ticket hasn't arrived" or "The hotel is overbooked."
We made a number of agreements with the girls for the Olympics. "How are we going to deal with the parents?" In Oman we decided that we wouldn't get involved with that side of things any more. Parents and boyfriends have to arrange tickets themselves; our manager can be the contact, but the players won't get involved. I did not set out to contact the parents myself, but I did explain the rules to parents who contacted me. Rules that the players themselves had determined. So you can use your influence for preparatory work and for shielding others. Winners have plans; losers have excuses.

If it's really important, you have to return to circle number one, to yourself. What do you see if things are not going well? Everyone goes to circle two, so you can always say that somebody else is to blame. "Yes, so-and-so didn't play well."
But what you really should be thinking at that moment is, "What did I do wrong? What could I have done better?"

The more you move to the outside, the less influence you can exert. Your goal is located outside the circles, and so you have to go through all the circles in order to reach it. And to achieve your goal, you will have to go through all the circles a second time because, having determined your plan, you have to return to yourself. You can't execute your plan until then.

7

THE CRISIS CLOCK KNOWS WHAT TIME IT IS

Every crisis that arises produces innovation. Eight years of preparing for Olympic gold produced a lot of innovations. But not just in technology and methods. The players in the team were 'refreshed' in the course of those years. You can't get out of a crisis if you carry on doing what you always did. Then you just get what you always got.
In many companies a crisis leads to a lull, sitting still while you're being fleeced. But sitting still doesn't get you anywhere. You won't be able to avoid doing things differently. Creativity is essential. Recognise the benefits of the crisis. For example, there is plenty of time available in organisations. Take the time to train people, to get to know more about particular aspects, things you never got round to before the crisis. Do something, in the knowledge that your competitors have the same problem.

The fact that we became world champions in 2006 produced another new crisis. No-one wanted to play friendlies against us any more during the preparations for Beijing. For example, we had a match planned against Australia in Oman but Australia cancelled it after the World Cup. That was another problem we had to deal with. How do you make sure you have enough practice games at the right level? That was when we started playing against boys, for example. Not the men's teams, but boys from the top-level youth teams. Good hockey players who had sufficient respect for the Dutch women's team not to behave like machos. All those lads were much bigger than the Dutch women's team. So the players really had to work hard physically. The girls complained too: "They sprint past us so easily. And they keep pushing us the whole time." Well, in that case the team will have to figure out how to deal with it: get better at backing people up. Push back.

If you just meekly take the punishment, you'll carry on taking it. If you give as good as you get sometimes, you won't have to take so much. Those matches were often close, narrowly won or lost. Very important matches in the preparations for China. Not only ideal for trying things out within the team, but also good for building up resistance. Later, in the final against China, we were ready for it when those strapping great Chinese girls came onto the pitch.

As a businessman, you often have to arrange competition for yourself in order to become stronger. Internal competition, challenging people to improve. Create your own crisis, as it were. Because that way you ensure you are better able to make your presence felt in the market, amongst the real competition.

Holland had had the best hockey players for twenty years, but not the best team. Arguments, discord, internal fighting. This may not have been visible because nobody talked about it. Girls do have a tendency to avoid conflict. They prefer to talk to someone else about it. They think you are better off not talking about it with your team because of the team spirit. Then they don't pass the ball to each other on the pitch because of some rumour or other. Exactly the wrong thing to do. Then I thought to myself: "I'm not going to be training nine times a week only to have a war break out during a tournament if we happen to draw. I'm going to make it something we can discuss." I was opening myself up by doing this, because sometimes it was me who was the subject of the discussion.

Of course the big advantage of the crisis in Beijing was that I already knew four years in advance when and where the crisis would take place: in August 2008 in China. You can see every crisis coming. Crisis is not random chance, crisis is a consequence. Crisis results in fear and fear is in your head. That was the case at the Den Bosch hockey club where I am the performance manager; I'm there to make the club better without deciding on their technical policy. I saw that at Chelsea when I was on a visit.

Frank Arnesen is the performance manager there. He is improving the club as a whole, as an organisation, and is making sure it innovates. That's what I am doing at Den Bosch. Back to the crisis. At the end of the 2008-2009 season, the men's first team was about to be relegated. They had already asked me a couple of times to share ideas with them and help out. The Den Bosch coach, Oriol Alcaraz, is an old mate of mine. He was my assistant when I was coaching the Spanish national team. In the end I agreed. The crisis was severe. I reckoned that the chance of relegation was more than fifty per cent. At the time, four internationals (three Argentineans and one German) were absent due to international commitments. On top of that, three other players were injured. They were scheduled to play four matches against the top four in the table. They lost heavily. And by the time all the internationals had returned, they were in a vicious circle. Den Bosch chose rightly not to break that vicious circle by getting rid of the coach. Oriol Alcaraz had already asked me to join them a couple of times but I had stalled. He was the coach, there was a technical director and two assistants. So I would be joining them as number five. What's more, I can be a bit of a know-all, so I thought they really didn't need me on board as well. When the committee pushed me to get involved as well, I got down to work with Oriol. I concentrated more on the psychological role, talking to players. They had to stop focusing on the result and get back to the process. No more working on new technical tricks for now – work on their mental resilience. It's not that we have to win, we have to put up a fight. "Inch by inch." Yes; I did indeed play Al Pacino again. And once again it was a roaring success. In addition, I shifted the responsibilities within the team back to the people they belonged to.

Four years in four weeks, crisis notebooks and putting things into perspective

At Den Bosch hockey club I did what I had done in four years in the run-up to Beijing in only four weeks. I showed them the flow model. They recognised their own situation. Recognition is acknowledgement, acknowledgement is acceptance. They understood the situation they were in. They didn't have the skills to match the challenge and vice versa. I put their minds at rest with that chart.

As a director you can also sometimes say to an employee, "I understand how you feel. I know what's going on in your mind." It's also a way of showing respect. I saw one of the Argentineans in Den Bosch burst into tears. For the first time, he was getting confirmation of the feeling of misery he had been walking around with for ages. Then I showed them all the goals they had scored before the winter break. All those lovely attacks and great moves. "Look, this is what you can do." That was how I showed them that the problem wasn't in how they played hockey but in their minds. It was purely a mental issue. I also showed them a clip of the first time we became champions as Den Bosch, in 1998, beating our arch-rivals Amsterdam. You could see me when I was still a player, running across the screen. And Dennis Dijkshoorn, the 37-year-old assistant coach who we were fielding as a player again despite his age because of all the injuries. So the players of Men's 1 saw him in the glory days of Den Bosch. That helped get rid of the doubts. I still remember how we – the players – had doubts then as well, in the play-offs against Amsterdam. "We can't do this, we'll never win," we said to each other. The keeper Ronald Jansen heard that and said: "Fine. If it's already settled, I'm off." He picked up his things and drove away from the ground. Then we discovered we were indeed talking ourselves into failure. We called Ronald, said he should come back and we won the national championship.

In the end Den Bosch didn't get relegated that season. The approach worked. I do hope that I didn't give the players some-

thing just for a few weeks, but for the rest of their careers. You only ever hear that later, if you hear it at all. Sometimes the Dutch women's team players say to me years later, "Yeah, I learned so much back then."
I will be honest with you: that does give me satisfaction.

The crisis has only ended when you have achieved your objective. But the feeling of crisis ends as soon as you are playing well, the tactics are right, your opponent starts to panic. If you as a company have to wait for a good feeling until the economic crisis has ended then you are in for a couple of tough years now. You need to figure out how to get rid of some of that feeling of crisis during the process, while you are on the road to recovery. Through the minor success stories, by making the changes work. If you can recognise it as a turnaround, then you are coming through the crisis. So show recognisable results, however minor. You don't need to win the match in order to show you are making progress.
See the crisis as a chance to get things back on the rails. If sales allow it, take a rest from all the hard work over the past few years when sales were increasing and profits rising year in year out. Read a book, take a course, sharpen your axe, and make sure you are alert again. Because before you know it, the crisis will have ended and you'll be fully immersed in work again.

I have a crisis notebook for every job I take on. I write everything down in it that I might otherwise forget. Often, that notebook is also a diary recording the developments you see in the team. Those notes show how you grow into a crisis and out of it again. So I had a crisis notebook for the 2004 Olympics and for the World Cup in 2002 and 2006, and of course one for the Olympics in China.
Managers and team leaders should keep a 'crisis notebook'. The notes in it only cover solutions for immediate problems. The overview that a crisis notebook like this gives you can make you aware of the course you are taking while you are still in the middle of a process.

If you land in a crisis, there comes a point when you start to doubt everything. As if the whole world around you is subsiding. That's because of your targets. It makes no sense to try to achieve targets during a crisis that were set before the crisis. Modify your targets, otherwise you will go crazy. If a car dealer has to meet sales targets in 2009 that are based on previous years... well, I wish him lots of luck, but he's going to be very unhappy for the next few years.

Adjust your targets, focus more on the relationships with your customers so that they are still with you when the economy recovers, even if they don't buy a new car from you this year.

It was boiling hot in China during the Games. But our opponents had that problem too. That means it's not about whether or not you can handle the heat, it's about whether you can cope with it better than the rest. Two years earlier in Madrid, we became world champions with a style of play that relied heavily on pressing, putting your opponent under tight pressure early on in the game. If we had tried that in China, our opponents would have wiped the floor with us. We couldn't do that there. So every crisis requires its own – objectives. Realistic ones. If the Dutch national team plays in 2012 with the same aims they had in China – punishing opponents for their errors with our penalty corners – then they won't get far. New objectives will have to be defined for the London Olympics.

In times of crisis you shouldn't merely adjust your goals so that they are a bit lower. You have to formulate new ones.
It is not enough just to lower your sales targets. You could go for keeping up employment levels, retaining knowledge. In a crisis that will be at the cost of profits. So if you go for the result, you will have to fire your experts. But if you fire all the people with professional know-how now in order to boost your profits, don't complain in three years' time that your competitors are making bigger profits than you because all your former experts are now working for them. Making your organisation durable is

a hot item during a crisis. Think about the longer term, rather than just about keeping profits as high as possible. I accepted a poorer result during the Champions Trophy in Germany in 2008; I went with a young team in order to spare the old hands, who had played a tough season plus play-offs. I could have gone to Germany with a stronger team, but then I would have had to accept a reduction in the durability of the team for Beijing. Of course, the hockey association asked me what I thought I was doing and why wasn't I taking my strongest team.

I said: "No, forget it. Which is more important: winning the Champions Trophy, which we've already won a few times, or winning at the Games? I'd really far rather be third or fourth in the Champions Trophy..."
In the end the Argentineans won the Champions Trophy and they went wild with joy. I saw my players watching, fuming: "When we play the Argentineans next time, we'll wipe them out."
So really I had achieved exactly what I wanted. We met Argentina at the Olympics in the semi-finals. We walloped them 5-2...

Where are you in the crisis? At what stage? The 'crisis clock' (on the following pages) shows what you have to do at each stage in the crisis.
In the short term, you can do most by working on the mental and tactical aspects. Technical and physical aspects are more for the longer term. If you are a company in a crisis and you have gone through your reserves, you have to get down to work now. Different tactics and marketing. Different mentality, sales techniques, discounts. If your company has built up enough of a reserve, you can allow yourself to take a much more long-term approach to this crisis. Put more time and effort into training, let employees swap duties, let employees collaborate.
In a construction company, the sales people had spent years selling projects that the designers (known as the project planners there) couldn't implement. In addition, these designers were in scarce supply and so they were badly overworked. There was al-

ways conflict between the two groups. The sales people sold things the designers couldn't produce and the designers produced things the sales people couldn't sell. Then the whole building sector landed in a crisis. In that company it was decided that the project engineers, the designers, should join in on the sales meetings for two months. Just like that, to see what happens there. They were able to use what they learned there directly in their drawings. That's the kind of insight you can get thanks to a crisis.

The crisis clock

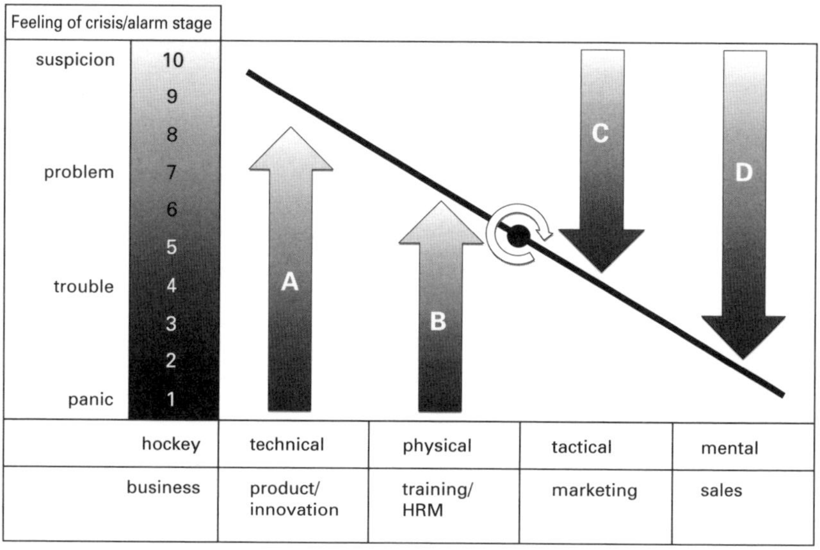

The question is: where is your company in the crisis? When the figure is in the white, the safe position of alarm stage 10, then the feeling of crisis is based on merely a suspicion. It is clear on the horizontal axis that there is plenty of room to focus on products and product innovation – what would be called technical aspects in the hockey world (arrow A). There is also room for training and HRM (Human Resource Management) aspects such as development plans (arrow B). As a hockey coach I would call that 'physical training' for fitness. If there is just a suspicion of a crisis, you don't need to work on tactics and mental aspects too much yet.

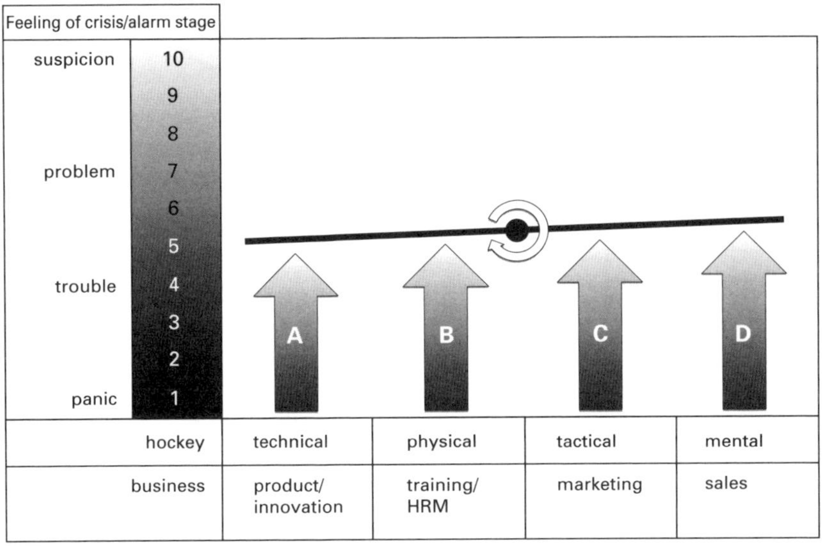

In the diagram above, the feeling of crisis has risen to 'trouble', alarm stage 5, in the grey zone. Now a company has to reallocate its efforts to product development (less), training (less), marketing (more) and sales (more). In hockey terms, this is a training camp a few weeks before a major tournament. You are still giving a reasonable amount of attention to technical and physical aspects, but you are also discussing tactical aspects and the first mental aspects are being considered.

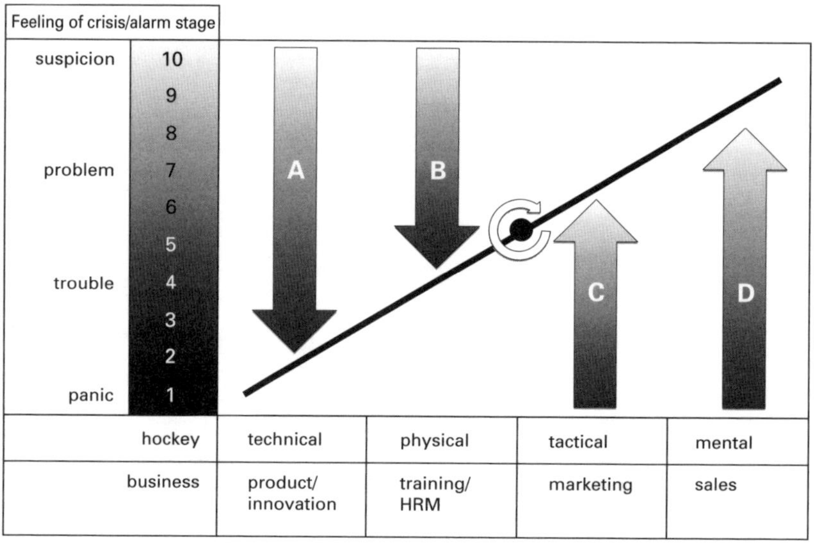

In this diagram, you have an emergency: alarm stage 1, panic! The pointer is right in the black. In this situation, there is no longer any point in fine-tuning the product or implementing an innovation. Training and developing people won't give you much breathing space either. All your efforts go on marketing (arrow A) and sales (arrow B).
As a hockey coach, I shouldn't still be talking about techniques for controlling the ball two hours before the Olympic final. Or doing a couple of extra physical sprinting exercises. I have to concentrate on the tactics they should use and I have to give my players mental strength, boost their morale.

So the crisis clock is a tool for deciding what your priorities should be at each stage in a crisis.

Opportunity 11: Decide where you are in the crisis

If you know where you are in the crisis, you also know what you have to do to get out of it. Check that regularly. As you slowly but surely come out of the crisis, you can begin to set different priorities.

I think a lot of companies need to regain awareness of their successes during a crisis. Prove there are things that you as a company can do well. It can give you confidence, or insights into a different approach. Some facts:

- History shows us that the average recession lasts 11.5 months.
- The foundation for the most profitable investments is laid during a recession.
- In the long term, acquisitions made by companies during a recession are forty per cent more successful than takeovers of companies during an economic boom.
- Marketing efforts are more effective during a recession.

The need for a crisis, the pain of winning

Would we have been Olympic champions in 2008 if we had won in Athens in 2004? I'll never be able to prove it, but I think we needed the crisis in 2004 in order to raise our game above our normal level in 2008. I would have preferred us to have won in Athens in 2004 and then lost the World Cup in 2006. Then that would have been the crisis we needed to become Olympic champions again in 2008. I know, I can hardly complain with all those titles we've won. And I'm not complaining. The crisis gave me the ultimate victory. The crisis was also the result of my worst low point. Perhaps that contrast makes the gold even better. At any rate the crisis made me more subdued. I'll never reach such a low point as I did in 2004. The euphoria in Beijing after the final was less than the euphoria after the semi-final we won in Athens. That's another thing that I say I'll never let happen again. The pain I felt after the defeat in 2004 is something I'll never feel again. Simply because I will no longer allow that pain. I don't have many enemies in my life. I got that from my father. Live and let live, each his own opinion. There are bound to be people who think I'm not a good coach. Fine. Irrelevant to me. But I'm not going to hold it against those people. I say "hello" to them. I think that's enough. The same journalists who slated me in their articles in 2004 were patting me on the back in 2008. Well, let's just say that they have a job to do as well.

I guess that players who criticised me strongly on the sports programmes may have had their reasons to do so. At least, that's how I think about it now, but I thought differently about it when I sat in front of the TV in 2004, of course...

You will only be willing to work on a crisis when you experience it first-hand. Of course, we saw the worldwide economic crisis coming. At the beginning of 2008, things were already happening that showed that a crisis was on the way. Yet we were only prepared to do anything about it in the Netherlands a year later. Which is logical. You have to feel the hurt. Until that moment, you somehow believe that the crisis won't affect you. It always happens to someone else.

I can look back on it now. Now I know that the three rest days in Athens affected us. We should have continued training rather than shopping and going to the beach. At that time I focused too much on our own shortcomings. I paid too much attention to the good sides of our opponents instead of their weaknesses. In Athens, I was afraid that my team would underestimate Germany in the final. That never happens, though – a top athlete simply wants to win the final. I had created too much tension. I can still hear myself saying to my team before the final, "This is what you've worked at for four years..."
It wasn't a smart thing to say. During the years of preparation we didn't rotate the team enough. My fixed starting eleven had become too critical; when exhaustion struck in Athens, it was already too late. I also failed to see that my coaching staff were not functioning as well as they could have. I should have been aware of that. That was a job for the manager, the coach, and I didn't do it properly at that time.
In Athens we had two apartments, two living rooms, for the entire group of players. It turned out that one apartment ended up with most of the players from Den Bosch, while the other had most of the players from Amsterdam.

Two camps. I thought that would be okay, but that was something else that didn't work.

We changed a lot during the preparations for Beijing as a result of that crisis. We kept changing the room assignments, made sure that the players came closer to each other, no matter what club they belonged to. We had two apartments again in Beijing too. But now we had one living room for us all. The other living room was used for physio treatments. It was no coincidence; it was the result of what we had learned from 2004. Minke Booij and Fatima Moreira de Melo were responsible for allocating team members' rooms – two of the players who had been in Athens too. Thanks to the Action Typing sessions, we were able to get opposite personalities together.

Even before the Olympics, I knew that I would quit after they were over. I had had enough of it after eight years. I informed the hockey association and told my team about this decision five months before Beijing. When I told them, they said to me that it would be wise for me not to announce it. I would certainly lose my credibility. I pointed out the ultimate target to everyone: winning gold at the Olympic Games. I'm sure that at that time none of my team members was thinking about the Dutch team *after* the Games. Announcing my departure made no difference.

Sometimes I wonder what made us win in China. It was the details. I spoke to someone from a car company. I had sympathy for him; I thought his business was going through bad times. To my surprise this entrepreneur was not complaining. "You should see how many cars more we are still selling than our competitors. It's because we stick to our promises. If we say that we'll call back the next day at three o'clock, we do call back the next day at three. If we promise our clients that they'll have our quotation the day after tomorrow, then they get our quotation in time. We bought a load of toys for the children's corner in the showroom. We know selling cars in times of crisis takes more time. So the

children have to be kept occupied for longer. They're just details, but they work."
And that's a fact.

I knew what other national teams' managers focused on. Australia had a manager who focused on details, just like me. I would tell my team that they had to respond to that. The Argentinean coach didn't focus on that at all, he didn't care about details. When I saw one of their cameramen with an old, analogue camera and no laptop, I knew they weren't keeping statistics of our matches, like we did of our opponents. During match discussions I could easily tell the team all the things that this opponent did not know about us. At a certain moment, team members like Minke Booij and Janneke Schopman were able to tell what penalty corner move Argentina were taking, based on the posture of their star player Aymar for that short corner. If she leaned on that stick, the ball would be pushed away. If she held her stick low down, she would be shooting the ball. Players shouted at each other, "Stick low, stick low! She's going to shoot!" Then Minke Booij came racing out of the goal and cleared the ball before Aymar could even strike it. Janneke Schopman could tell from the positioning of the Argentinean stopper's feet which side the ball would go to. If you know specifics like these, you'll win on the details. But it's also because of the perfectionism of those players. Argentina weren't clever enough to take advantage of that: getting Aymar to lean on her stick but then still shoot after all. Australia were smart enough, but we knew that too...

I went through a very tough time after the Athens Olympics. The media savaged my reputation: "Without those excellent players, Lammers would not even have reached the last four" and stuff like that. We played the semi-final against Argentina on the first anniversary of my mother's death. I felt that it was as if my mother had helped me get those penalties. All those emotions resulted in a dramatic explosion during the final.

After losing the final, I even wondered whether my life would have any point again after such a miserable crisis. I'm going back to my mother, I thought.

The nicest thing about a crisis is looking back on it. And being able to think, "Did I make such a fuss over it back then?" In fact, in a crisis you should be able to realise that you'll learn a lot from it afterwards, and that it will prove useful. And that it will have been another opportunity.
You can hear a lot of people now saying, "It's a good thing that people are rocking the boat hard now. This economic crisis is an inevitable correction for everything that went wrong over recent years."
Although this doesn't put an end to the crisis, it reduces the tension and stress to an acceptable level.
If you're prepared to shoulder part of the blame in the middle of a crisis, you will be able to look back on the crisis with more satisfaction. I took the blame for the lost final in 2004; I never blamed anyone else but myself.

It caused a crisis for me immediately after we won in China. Did I enjoy the gold medal in China? Athens still bothers me. After the final in China, my first thought was: "Shit, this could have been my second..."
But on the other hand, part of the reason why we won in 2008 was that I did not want to go through the pain of losing an Olympic final again. That's why we prepared ourselves so thoroughly and that's why we focused on details. Perhaps we wouldn't have won in Beijing if we had won gold in Athens, who knows? It's guesswork. But I do know that (for me) the fear of losing and the will to win were important motivators on the road to the gold medal. My crisis is over. And I enjoyed it.

What I did with the Al Pacino film clip is what companies and organisations do with me. They hire me to make them confront themselves. To provide new insights. Because outsiders are often capable of 'forcing' you to move in the right direction.

Without knowing the details, I can give examples that correspond to developments within that particular company. I can make comparisons with sport that really make them face some home truths. I can give them something to think about. Preferably outside the box. On top of that, I can tell them things not only about the company and its staff, but about management too. That's what makes it so fascinating for my audience. There are so many similarities between top-level sport and entrepreneurship, managing a sports team and running a company, or being one of the sports team and one of the staff.

A word of thanks

Thanks for all the crises. They taught me a great deal, which only made me stronger. It's something that would be good for anyone who reads this book. You never beat a crisis, so don't try to do so. You must beat your competitors. I would like to thank everyone who made an appearance in this book. They all gave me something on my way to the final victory.

The Dutch team made me proud. I'm proud of sixteen girls who were prepared to push the boundaries. My coaching staff were a mirror and a sounding board for me, for which I would like to thank the team manager Sandra le Poole in particular. Physiotherapists Peter Verzijden and Johannes Veen: thank you for your dedication and for the fun we had. Assistant coaches Bart Looije and Max Caldas: your support and your calmness were indispensable. Our team physician, Irene Engelbertink, gave me peace of mind. Video analyst Lars Gillhaus gave me irritated eyes, for which I'm grateful... Our mental coach Rico Schuijers gave me the power to believe in myself; exercise physiologist Jos Geijsel gave me strength; our expert Toon Siepman gave me the winning penalty corner. I'd also like to thank the board of the hockey association for the confidence they showed in me, even when I chose my own path.

This book includes beautiful pictures full of memories. For these, I would like to thank Ben Haeck and Jeroen van Bergen. I would also like to thank Roel van Veen of Tirion for giving me another opportunity to write a book. Stanley Macnack, Jos Couwenberg, Pieter Pelt and Wim Kemps read this book before you, even before it was published. Their valuable advice and suggestions made the story even more complete. Thanks for your commitment and for your constructive way of thinking along with me.

Business consultant Ton Hendrickx compensated for my dyslectic B-minus with his communicative A-plus, recording everything that came up during our fascinating discussions. My thanks to the true writer, the ghost-writer of this book for his knowledge and expertise, in particular for the challenge of making comparisons outside the world of hockey.

I would like to thank my father for his indispensable warmth, my children Peppe and Jurre for putting things into perspective and for the fun that we have together, and finally I would like to thank my wife Karin: thank you for everything.